Getting Your Breath Back After Life Knocks It Out of You

Getting Your Breath Back After Life Knocks It Out of You

A Transparent Journey of Seeking
God through Grief

K.B.H. Niles

WESTBOW
PRESS
A DIVISION OF THOMAS NELSON

IMPORTANT: The information and advice in this book reflects the author's opinions and life experiences and is not intended to replace the counsel, advice, and/or services of trained professionals. Some may or may not have similar experiences with their grief or wellness process. Any mental, emotional, spiritual, dietary, or physical self-improvement should be discussed with a trained professional before making any changes. Dietary changes and exercise should always be undertaken with careful consideration and you are advised to consult with a health care professional before initiating any new wellness endeavors, especially if you are pregnant, overweight, or have other special conditions. In regards to all matters relating to your mental, emotional, physical, spiritual, and overall health or wellness, consulting an appropriate trained medical or mental health professional is advised.

WestBow Press books may be ordered through booksellers or by contacting:

WestBow Press
A Division of Thomas Nelson
1663 Liberty Drive
Bloomington, IN 47403
www.westbowpress.com
1-(866) 928-1240

ISBN: 978-1-4497-2560-0 (e)
ISBN: 978-1-4497-2561-7 (sc)
ISBN: 978-1-4497-2562-4 (hc)

Library of Congress Control Number: 2011914949

Printed in the United States of America
WestBow Press rev. date: 09/28/2011

I dedicate this book to my Heavenly Father and family. I never could have made it out of my darkest days without their incredible love, encouragement, and support. I am so grateful to each of them for helping me get my breath back after life knocked it out of me.

Contents

Introduction.. xi

Chapter 1 ~ The Day I Lost My Oxygen.....................................1

Chapter 2 ~ The Oxygen of Seeking God 9

Chapter 3 ~ The Oxygen of Encouragement............................29

Chapter 4 ~ The Oxygen of Gratefulness, Thankfulness,
and Praise..43

Chapter 5 ~ The Oxygen of Uniqueness 61

Chapter 6 ~ The Oxygen of Faith & Hope 71

Chapter 7 ~ The Oxygen of Relationships & Community 89

Chapter 8 ~ The Oxygen of Time...109

Chapter 9 ~ The Oxygen of Forgiveness..................................123

Chapter 10 ~ The Oxygen of Enjoying Life Through
Traditions & Wellness..139

End Matter/Appendices 161

Introduction

Written in memory and honor of my sister, dad, and loved ones, *Getting Your Breath Back After Life Knocks It Out of You* transparently shares my experiences with loss—and tells my personal testimony of how God restored my broken heart from the horrendous pain and emptiness of grief.

After going through the deaths of my dad, sister, four grandparents, two uncles, an aunt, two separate fiancés of my sister, and other family members and friends, as well as other challenges and heartaches, I began journaling my feelings and researched God's Word on grief, trials, and loss. I am by no means an expert on grief or grief recovery. I only know what I have personally experienced and what I have learned through God's Word. Over and over in the Bible, I found that God is rich in compassion and He desires for each of us to enjoy an extremely close relationship with Him. He also desires for each of us to learn to reverently fear, revere, love, and worship Him, even while going through the fiery trials of grief. When we run to Him, we finally come to the place of knowing that He is dependable and faithful—regardless of what we are going through. There are treasures to be gleaned, compassion from God to be revealed, and a deep genuine love experience with Him to be blessed with as we fall into the arms of God during times of grief, heartache, and loss.

Although very difficult to go through, grief is one of the most powerful teachers God can allow us to learn from. Throughout His Word, God has designed beautiful blueprints for grief and loss recovery with the purpose of guiding us through life difficulties. The Bible shares with us that life will be filled with loss, and heartbreaking hardships will be inevitable, but life will also be filled with blessings and joy. Our lives are intricately designed, created, and planned by God. He has a design, purpose, and a specific plan for every person which He reveals through a close relationship with Him.

At times, God's design, purpose, and plan for our lives is very favorable, while other times it is not. Ecclesiastes 3:1-14 shares we each will have times of joy, sorrow, gain, loss, peace, and conflict in our lives. Each life lesson, whether in favor or grief, is designed so we will have a better understanding of who God is through drawing close to His heart. As we develop a deeper relationship with Him, we learn how to love and serve Him more, as He reveals His plans and purpose for our lives.

God truly makes everything beautiful in His time once we realize and submit to the plans He has for our lives. When it feels as though your grief will never end, as though God has turned His eyes away from your pain, or that He has not heard your cries, please realize that He *is* there and He *will* reveal His ultimate purpose for your life. God will help you get the breath back that life knocked out of you as you seek Him with your whole heart.

Throughout my times of grief and loss, God has shown me time and time again how to get my breath back after life has knocked it out of me. As I have deepened my friendship with Him through my experiences with grief, He has been so faithful to restore my "breathing" ability.

Each chapter of *Getting Your Breath Back After Life Knocks It Out of You* reveals the Oxygens God has most used to help me "catch my breath," heal my heart, and restore my ability to live, love, and enjoy life once again.

In Ecclesiastes 3:1-14, God reveals a time and purpose for everything under the heavens that will affect each and every life. Some events in life are positive and pleasant while some are negative and heartbreaking. God desires to heal each broken heart and to draw close to every person. He desires for you to fully experience His love and compassion. Experiencing God's mercy, compassion, and love in a fresh new way will become a reality as you seek Him throughout your grief.

As you learn to seek God with your whole heart, He will carry you as you make the transition from being Grief-controlled into the beauty of being God-guided throughout your grief process. It is through being guided by God you will find the Oxygen you need to recover from grief. I pray you will find God's peace, comfort, and joy in spite of your heartbreaking pain. May God touch your heart and life in a way that truly comforts you, as He restores your soul and truly heals your broken heart. I have found that He is the ultimate Way of *getting your breath back after life knocks it out of you.*

Ecclesiastes 3:1-14, *"TO EVERYTHING there is a season, and a time for every matter or purpose under heaven:*

A time to be born and a time to die,
a time to plant and a time to pluck up what is planted,
A time to kill and a time to heal,
a time to break down and a time to build up,
A time to weep and a time to laugh,
a time to mourn and a time to dance,
A time to cast away stones and a time to gather stones together,
a time to embrace and a time to refrain from embracing,
A time to get and a time to lose,
a time to keep and a time to cast away,
A time to rend and a time to sew,
a time to keep silence and a time to speak,
A time to love and a time to hate,
a time for war and a time for peace.

What profit remains for the worker from his toil? I have seen the painful labor and exertion and miserable business which God has given to the sons of men with which to exercise and busy themselves. He has made everything beautiful in its time. He also has planted eternity in men's hearts and minds [a divinely implanted sense of a purpose working through the ages which nothing under the sun but God alone can satisfy], yet so that men cannot find out what God has done from the beginning to the end. I know that there is nothing better for them than to be glad and to get and do good as long as they live; And also that every man should eat and drink and enjoy the good of all his labor—it is the gift of God. I know that whatever God does, it endures forever; nothing can be added to it nor anything taken from it. And God does it so that men will [reverently] fear Him [revere and worship Him, knowing that He is]." (AMP)

CHAPTER 1

~

The Day I Lost
My Oxygen

"I'm sorry, but there was nothing we could do . . . she's gone," the doctor stated in a professional tone of voice on that life changing Thanksgiving morning.

I felt as though my stomach and heart had been knocked out of me, then after the initial shock, as though I couldn't breathe at all. My mind started spinning as grief, fear, shock, and anguish gripped my heart, *"No . . . I don't understand! She was supposed to come home later today! She wasn't even that sick . . . she's only not felt well for a couple of weeks . . . she's only 22!"*

I immediately started crying and praying, hoping against all hope that God would somehow perform a miracle, wishing that I could rewind time, or that all of this could just go away. Sadly, that isn't how life worked out on that cold Thanksgiving.

Thanksgiving had always been a holiday filled with joy, love, gratefulness, and great celebration for our family. As I began to slowly walk to my sister's hospital room to view her lifeless body, all of the familiar holiday feelings of joy, love, gratefulness, and celebration were now being replaced with intense grief, anxiety, and heartache with each and every dreaded step that I took. Instead of enjoying Thanksgiving dinner together, making new memories, taking family pictures, and celebrating Thanksgiving like we always had as a family, we each began the process of being ripped wide open emotionally, raw with fresh grief . . . again.

I had already experienced the devastating deaths of my dad, grandparents, other family members, and several friends while growing up—and our family was currently in mourning because my other sister's fiancé had just died three weeks before our oldest sister's death. Grief had certainly written many stories in our family, but no previous loss could have possibly prepared us for my sister's death.

Everybody has a grief story that begins the very moment death or loss hits them as they are catapulted into a grief experience they didn't sign up for. After we heard a code blue initiated on the overhead ICU intercom, my sister's death catapulted me into a heartbreaking grief experience that has been one of the hardest grief stories to unfold in my life. My sister had been in the hospital for only a few days, after having what seemed to be severe allergies, so we were genuinely shocked to hear *her* room number attached to a code blue. I can not adequately describe the panic, confusion, concern, and heartbreak I felt the very moment I heard her room number called.

This wasn't the first code blue we had heard that Fall morning. After hearing each code blue, I prayed for the unknown families and felt so sorry for their heartache, especially since it was a holiday. Then I heard the code blue that jolted our lives into a downward spiral of grief because the defining code blue wasn't coded to an anonymous room, to some anonymous unknown stranger—this defining code blue was coded to my sister's room.

After hearing her code blue, I silently hoped that there had been a mistake, that maybe someone had coded the wrong room number. The wait was agonizing and we kept anticipating the doctor coming to the waiting room to say she was alright, that they had revived her. As we watched her doctor slowly walking towards us, the news we were given was heartbreakingly opposite of what we had hoped and prayed fervently to hear.

Immediately after being told of my sister's death, I didn't think it was possible to contain my excruciating pain and sorrow, but I had no privacy . . . and I also had no choice. I wanted to scream and cry out in anguish, but only tears would surface. As I began to process the new reality of her death, my heart sunk with each and every step as I made my way to see her one last time. The pain was unbelievable as I approached her hospital room, realizing as I walked in that she wouldn't be alive . . . knowing she wouldn't respond . . . realizing I would never have another conversation with her . . . I'd never feel a hug from her again . . . or see her face light up with her little smile that I loved seeing every time I saw her . . . I would never have the opportunity to do anything with her ever again. All of the things we were planning to do were now gone. All of the things we had talked about doing in the future would never be. The special days we had been planning and preparing for would now never be anything more than a vapor. *Anything the future could have held, suddenly and permanently vanished without warning.*

As I walked into my sister's room, my heart was divided. I wanted to run to my sister and hug her, but my heart also wanted to run as far away from this new situation that I felt thoroughly unprepared for. I apprehensively walked in, sat beside my sister on her hospital bed, and gently held my sister's hand. I was surprised that her hand was still so soft and warm. Her hair was soaking wet from trying hard to stay here on earth. The warmth of her body was cruel, making it seem as though she was still alive. I wanted to comfort her . . . but she wasn't *here* to comfort. I noticed that my sister had several freshly applied thick bandages under her collarbone as I was about to hug her for the last time. What had she been through that morning during the code blue? Why did they have to cut into her chest? What suddenly happened that caused her to die . . . instead of possibly coming home later that day to celebrate Thanksgiving as her doctor had anticipated? I felt as though I was in a nightmare with no exit. Studying her face, I could see she had been through a lot of panic and pain. She looked stressed, saddened, and not at peace which broke my heart for her. I was devastated that she died without having loved ones around her. My sister hated being alone when she was sick or in any medical situation. Why hadn't the hospital staff allowed any of us to go back to see her after she had just asked them to call us to come be with her? Frozen in a heartbroken trance of confusion, I mindlessly and automatically did what I had always done when she needed me . . . I rubbed her face.

My sister always loved having her face rubbed (or "painted" as she called it), especially when she didn't feel well. As I gently painted her face with my fingertips for the very last time, I was pierced with a sorrow indescribable, and my heart began flooding with a mixture of extreme grief, guilt, and regret as hot tears streamed down my face. Too much reality was mixed with my uninvited grief. It was real enough to stab every ounce of my being with a deep pain that I had never felt before, yet it was surreal as though I had become frozen in time. The pain was uncomfortable and unbearable rendering me speechless.

As I held my sister's hand and rubbed her face, the story of Lazarus came to mind. Through my tears, I began bargaining with God—begging Him again with my entire heart to do a miracle by somehow having her start breathing again. When I realized that God wasn't going to revive her, I begged Him to let me take her place. I immediately felt sick to my stomach as remorse, regret, and guilt flooded my heart. Why hadn't I made the time to visit her while she had been in the hospital the past few days? Why didn't I arrive at the hospital just a little bit earlier before she died so I could have seen her . . . talked to her . . . told her how much I loved her . . . hugged her . . . and painted her face to comfort her? Why did I spend the previous night going to a Thanksgiving church banquet? Why did I go home after the banquet to make Thanksgiving pies and treats to surprise her . . . instead of simply going to see her? Why hadn't I realized just how sick she really was? Why didn't I drop everything I was doing to rub her shoulders and paint her face like she had asked me to the last day I was with her? A few days before she was hospitalized, I had stopped by her house. After talking on her front porch, she had invited me to come inside to talk to her, she said she needed to tell me something, but I didn't because I had plans to meet my boyfriend at the mall. Why didn't I drop everything to talk to her? I will now never know what she needed to tell me that day. What seemed unimportant at the time ended up being of great importance and now haunted me. My guilt was now competing with my grief and the anguishing regret I felt was miserable. How could I have made so many shallow, selfish, foolish decisions the last days of her life? I had no idea how limited her days were. She was so young that serious illness or death didn't even enter my mind as possibilities. I thought that I would have all the opportunity in the world to spend time with her.

Death is so intrusive and final, destroying every future opportunity and possibility. I wanted so much more time with my sister and the finality of knowing she was dead was more than I could take.

Still holding my sister's hand, I forced my mind to change gears and began to remember that precious last day I had spent with her at our mom's house. Although I could tell my sister was tired and didn't feel well, she was still so full of life. She was in such a good mood as she talked about how she and her husband were going to try to have another baby. God had already blessed her with three wonderful daughters that she adored, and she really wanted to try to give her husband a son. After she finished talking about her girls and husband, I remember confiding in her of how my boyfriend and I had looked at engagement rings at the mall the day before. She was so happy when I asked her to be my matron of honor and for her daughters to be my flower girls in my wedding. She gave me a big hug then asked me to let her be the first to know when my wedding date was going to be. She wanted to be sure to lose any pregnancy weight and look great in her matron of honor dress. As she happily talked about her daughters and the prospect of another baby, her face lit up just like it always did when she talked about being a mom.

Motherhood had certainly agreed with my sister, complementing her fun-loving personality and sensitive loving heart. My sister loved to have fun with those she loved. One of her most endearing trademarks was how she loved having fun and playing practical jokes. In fact, if there could have been a queen of fun or practical jokes, she would have been royalty for sure. The great thing about my sister's personality was how she balanced fun with sentimentality. She was a super fun person, but she also had a heart of gold. Every holiday, she would buy Hallmark cards to let all of her family know how much she cared. If she took someone to the airport, she'd be the one to cry and hug you really big. She had an amazing heart.

After remembering that treasured last day I spent with my sister, so many other special memories of my sister and our siblings began to pour into my mind as I sat beside her. She and my other siblings had made growing up together so much fun. My sister's fun nature continued into her short-lived adult years as well, she was all about making memories with loved ones. Two months before she died, my sister had planned a vacation with my mom for all of our family—we had all enjoyed what was to be, unknown to us, our last family vacation with her. Reflecting on all of our good memories and vacations . . . and realizing there would never be an opportunity for new ones . . . I pleaded with God for a miracle one last time. My grief began cementing as I realized that there would be no miracle that day. She laid there, still warm as if still so full of life, but there was no life. After the initial shock and pain solidified, my grief grew numb yet consumed me.

In the months after that sorrowful Thanksgiving of my sister dying, as I was trying to make sense of my sister's death, it really hit home how much she meant to me. We had always shared an extraordinary bond, as our family has always been very close. Reflecting on what my sister's life meant to me, I realized that had it not been for her, I wouldn't even be alive. Without my sister, I would have died when I was twelve. As my grief settled in, while thinking about her life and death, the guilt that I felt from *my* ability to still breathe, laugh, love and live when she couldn't was excruciating . . . and the guilt that I felt from being able to hug, hold, love, and spend time with her daughters when she couldn't was bittersweet at times. I continued to enjoy and love my time with my nieces, but it felt so cruel that I was blessed to be a part of their lives when their own mother wasn't.

I dreaded the grief and guilt that I felt from my sister's death. I felt so much pain in my soul, the innermost part of my heart that I could feel in the pit of my being. I sank into a deep depression and became desperate to find any way to feel better . . . or at least feel any sense of normalcy again. The depression was there when I woke up in the morning and it remained there when I'd fall asleep at night—if I could sleep at all. I felt as though something bad was going to happen, as though someone else was going to die. I felt unbalanced and didn't understand how to stabilize my soul to find relief. I had been through deaths, trials, and heartaches in life before, but nothing ever could have prepared me for the devastating and sudden loss of my sister. I felt like I was losing my mind at times.

I simply wasn't prepared for my grief—not that anyone ever truly is. I had so many plans with my sister, never contemplating that those plans would never come to be. Grief had ripped those plans away permanently. While going through the heartache of my sister's death, it felt as though grief had ripped my heart out and was holding it hostage. I began to hate and resent my grief to its very core. I found that the worst part of grief was that it was in control. Grief wasn't something that I could shut off or decide to not go through. I knew from past experience that it would have to play out in its own timing . . . but this time felt different. I knew right away that this was going to be one of the hardest times of my life and it was going to take a toll on our family. I was heartbroken for my mom and worried about her. My oldest sister was named after my mom and they enjoyed an extremely close relationship and bond—so close that they talked several times a day on the phone. I also was very concerned for my other sister because we were still mourning the loss of her fiancé who had died only three weeks before our sister. I knew how horrible I felt, but I couldn't even imagine or comprehend how compounded my mom's grief or my other sister's grief must be. I watched my sister suffer through her tears and I felt helpless that I couldn't relieve her grief. I saw my mom go from a vibrant woman who smiled all of the time to being a mother crushed by the death of her daughter. My sister's daughters were confused as they could barely comprehend Heaven . . . and my heart broke when they asked why their mommy had to go there. They loved and missed their mom very much, I felt helpless when they would ask if there was any way to visit her in Heaven.

They say that if there has been previous grief, it can resurface when triggered by new grief. I found this to be very true. My sister's death brought to the surface all of the feelings I had buried from previous deaths, losses, and past hurts. I missed my sister terribly and missed being able to talk to her as I had talked to her every day. She was the one I had always confided in about everything. Who was I going to call every time something good or bad happened? Who was I going to talk to when I needed advice or needed to vent? Little did I know that God was paving the way for me to be totally dependent on nobody but Him. He was about to teach me many lessons about grief, loss, and life. My sister's death (and any previous loss) was just the beginning. God was about to take me on a custom designed grief experience with only Him so that He could teach me how to get my breath back that life had knocked out of me.

CHAPTER 2

~

The Oxygen of
Seeking God

Psalm 34:17-18, *"Is anyone crying for help? God is listening, ready to rescue you. If your heart is broken, you'll find God right there; if you're kicked in the gut, he'll help you catch your breath."* (MSG)

Everybody will experience grief, loss, and life challenges during the course of their lifetime. Most are unprepared for their grief and the impact it will have. Grief is brutal and has a way of making you feel as though everything great in your life is slowly being crushed, leaving you gasping for air. If you're reading this book right now, I imagine that you have had the breath knocked out of you and you are desperately trying to find any sense or hope in the heartache or loss you are facing.

After going through the loss of multiple loved ones, I remember each time trying to find anything that could offer me help or hope. In my quest to finding help after my sister's death, I purchased some books on grief recovery. After reading several grief recovery books and studying the grief steps, I was left frustrated and more confused as they offered no real help or hope for me personally. The books seemed to offer worldly or psychological ways of getting through grief, but none of the books I had read addressed my spiritual needs. In my frustration, I cried out to God for answers and pleaded with Him to heal my grieving broken spirit and heart. Shortly after crying out to Him, He began to reveal truths to my heart as I read His Word, and I began soaking up anything related to grief that I could find in the Bible. I began journaling my ideas, feelings, scriptures, and anything else regarding my experience with grief which lead to the writing of this book to encourage others who are going through grief. I decided to write a grief recovery book because I felt that if I was left frustrated and confused, then surely someone else needed to discover a different way to grieve too—a way that included God.

Psalm 70:5, *"I am afflicted and needy; hurry to me, God. You are my help and my deliverer; LORD, do not delay."* (HCSB)

Everybody has a life story as well as a life purpose. When one goes through loss, the valuable opportunity to understand, know, and love God better, as well as learn how to live a fuller life, immediately begins. My life story has been filled with heartaches, trials, and grief, but through my grief and loss experiences, I have discovered what hope truly is, as well as my life purpose. It would have been very easy to have grown bitter, due to the life changing circumstances I have been through, but God had a different plan. In His great love, compassion, consolation, and mercy, He has shown me how to get my joy and breath back in spite of life knocking it out of me time and time again. God truly is amazing at consoling a broken heart. As you open your heart to seek and trust Him throughout your grief, there is a precious joy that He shares and blesses you with. Psalm 94:19, *"When anxiety was great within me, your consolation brought me joy."* (NIV)

The road to healing is never an easy one. Anyone who has been affected by grief knows firsthand how horrifically heartbreaking loss is to go through. Feeling as though you are dead but can't die is a reality to those who have experienced deep grief or loss. Grief is merciless to the one going through it, but God is there to balance you and raise you up. He is such an amazing source of stability when everything around you has fallen apart. It is normal to feel as though you are falling apart when traumatized by grief. You may think, do, or say things that are uncharacteristic or unexpected. Depending on the severity of your grief, you may not feel like yourself for a period of time. You may even feel like you're going crazy. It takes time for a heart, mind, and spirit to balance out after going through intense grief.

Losing anyone or anything of great value that was special and meant the world to you is always confusing and painful. You are likely to feel an overwhelming variety of unpredictable emotions. You may feel lost, confused, sad, angry, depressed, maybe even desperate. Desperate to feel better . . . desperate to feel dead . . . desperate to feel alive . . . desperate to feel anything other than your grief and pain. When going through loss, you quickly find you are not in control, which adds to the already present pain, desperation, and confusion. The loss you are facing may have been something within your control or something totally out of your control. The principles offered in this book are universal, in that these principles are helpful for various situations of loss.

Each person has an expertise in whatever loss they have faced. Your loss expertise may be the death of a loved one, the death of a marriage or other key relationship, the death of losing a prized goal, plan, or dream, the death of your career or finances, not having someone accept or love you from a key person that was supposed to have (such as a spouse, parent, stepparent, in-law, or other family member), or perhaps your loss expertise may be the shattering of your self worth due to emotional, verbal, physical, or sexual abuse. You may have gone through the heartache of a child's death, a stillborn child, a miscarriage, or infertility. Maybe you are going through a child or family member's rebellion, substance abuse, or suicide. You may be in anguishing regret and grieving an abortion. Perhaps you are in the military and are deeply struggling with the realities you face everyday: the daily reality of your mortality, the death of a fellow soldier, a troubled marriage, or other situations of loss.

There are various situations of grief and loss. Your loss may have just happened or may have occurred several years ago. Although everybody grieves differently, the principles of grief recovery are universal and can be helpful for various situations. Grief recovery is also beneficial for past loss as well, even if the loss occurred years ago.

It is my prayer that as you read this book, God will touch your heart and life in a way that comforts you, as He restores your soul and heals your broken heart as only He can. He is the ultimate way of getting your breath back after life knocks it out of you, providing you with strength.

1 Peter 5:10, *"And the God of all grace, who called you to his eternal glory in Christ, after you have suffered a little while, will himself restore you and make you strong, firm and steadfast."* (NIV)

In honor and memory of my sister, dad, and loved ones, I have written this book as a way of helping others go from the horrendous pain and emptiness that a heart feels from grief, trials, and loss, into the arms of a loving merciful God. You may not see God as loving or merciful right now, you may even feel as though God has abandoned you, but please realize that simply is not true. He is right there in the midst of your pain, waiting to heal your broken heart, desiring to help you pick up the pieces of your shattered heart, hope, and life.

While going through grief, I talked with various family members about their individual grief and the heartaches they had experienced. Majority went through multiple feelings. Some had feelings of anger and reported times of questioning God, so if you are struggling with God, that's alright. He loves you and *He is faithful to meet you right where you are.*

Throughout this book, I'm going to share with you stories of how my family has effectively dealt with loss and grief from various situations in life. The stories that I share with you are from individuals that are very dear to my heart. Their stories reveal how grief, life lessons learned the hard way, and ultimately God's healing have had a great impression and impact on their life. In some circumstances, *grief has even given their life purpose a deeper meaning, as well as a greater impact, than had they lived a perfect life void of pain and loss.* I also will share with you my experiences of learning to heal, to not merely survive by going through the motions, but to actually have the ability to smile again and to be able to laugh and truly live life without feeling guilty for doing so.

It sounds so easy on paper but in all reality, the lessons I have learned during times of grief have been the hardest lessons I have ever had to learn. They have also been the most rewarding in that I have learned more about God, myself, and others than had I never experienced grief or loss.

With God's help, you can begin the healing process and finally find peace, comfort, love, and hope so you are able to breathe again. It's time for you to get your breath back, so take comfort. Before you begin reading the rest of this book, take a moment right now and ask God to grant you wisdom, understanding, and grace. Ask Him to drench you with His love, comfort, and mercy. Ask Him to reveal to you how best to get your breath and life back.

You may be concerned that you will never be able to heal. I didn't think I would ever heal from certain situations of loss, but I have experienced His healing power, and have seen God miraculously heal other hurting hearts time and time again. You will find that after life knocks the breath out of you, God is so faithful to be your oxygen until He fills you back with His beautiful gift of true breath and life. You may just be a prayer away from finally feeling the beginning of the relief and healing you desire and deserve. Invite God to lead you through your grief, asking Him to walk closely beside you. He is the One who holds the key to healing your broken heart and shattered life—He is the only One who can truly show you how to get your breath back after life has knocked it out of you. I will warn you that some may try to get through their grief on their own, but those efforts will ultimately be in vain. I tried for many years to get my breath back on my own, to fill my life with what I thought would bring me relief from my pain, but nothing and no one was able to give me the *longterm* peace, comfort, relief, and help my heart needed until I allowed God to guide me through my grief recovery. God allows family, friends, professionals, books, programs, organizations, and support groups to be effective tools in grief recovery, *but healing ultimately comes from Him.* He created every heart, knows each heart inside and out, and knows *exactly* what it will take for true long-lasting healing to occur.

Everybody has a starting point in the grief journey they will take during the course of their life. To some, my experiences with loss and grief will seem big. To others, my experiences will seem small. Some have horribly big burdens to carry, while others carry smaller amounts of loss, but with each and every loss, grief hurts so very badly to the one going through their individual heartache. No two grief experiences are the same because everybody feels and processes their loss very differently and uniquely.

I truly believe that God allows grief (not *causes,* but *allows* grief) to become a part of our lives because of the rich lessons one can learn through times of bereavement. God's purpose for each person is and has always been the same: *that we worship, revere, and love Him and that we love and serve others.* We were created exclusively for Him, to learn to love Him more everyday, to prepare each of us for our life purpose as well as the role we will have for eternity. If we view our grief from a worldly perspective, we will become discouraged, disheartened, depressed, and possibly angry or bitter towards God, life, and those around us. It is of utmost importance that we all realize that nothing happens in life without first being sifted through God's will for His greater purpose and plans. If something has happened . . . be it good or bad . . . it is because He allowed it. If He allowed it, we can trust Him to work it out for His and our ultimate good: Romans 8:28, *"And we know that in all things God works for the good of those who love him, who have been called according to his purpose."* (NIV)

Please do not be mistaken or misunderstand. God most certainly does not enjoy allowing grief to be a part of our lives and He doesn't willingly bring grief or affliction upon anybody: Lamentations 3:31-33, *"For no one is cast off by the Lord forever. Though He brings grief, he will show compassion, so great is his unfailing love. For He does not willingly bring affliction or grief to anyone."* (NIV) If God allows a situation of grief to unfold in your life, He will be faithful to shower you with His compassion and unfailing love . . . He will be faithful to lead you through your grief.

Every heartache you go through in life opens up more opportunities for you to know God fuller, better, and more intimately in a way you would never have experienced had you never gone through grief or loss. The greatest treasure I have discovered through times of grief is a deeper relationship and friendship with God. As I have writhed in heartbreaking grief, God has been very faithful to heal my heart as I sought to be a "student" of God's: studying what delights Him through reading His Word, seeking to know more about His heart and nature, and studying His blueprints for grief has taught me so much about life, Heaven, and His love. I also have learned through very challenging situations to trust Him more and to rely on Him for strength. He has been so faithful to reveal truths to my heart, shower me with His love, and drench me in His grace.

It wasn't always like this though, I previously was not very enthusiastic about God. To be honest, it has been a process, and I fought off God's love and His help at first. I was extremely angry with God—I didn't think it was fair to go through the devastating deaths of my dad, sister, three of my grandparents, my boyfriend, and other friends, as well as being assaulted and other life trials, all before my 20th birthday. I felt like God was picking on my family or failing to protect us. I was confused as to why the majority of my friends had hardly experienced loss, but my family seemed to not be able to escape it. I viewed God as uncaring, merciless, uninvolved, detached, game-playing, and far away.

When you go through grief or loss, the question that is usually most demanded is, "Why?" or "Why me?" As I worked through these desperately hard questions, I discovered in God's Word that no one is exempt from trials in life. *Grief and loss are not respecters of anyone.* Matthew 5:45 says, *" . . . for He causes His sun to rise on the evil and the good, and sends rain on the righteous and the unrighteous."* (NASB) Blessing, as well as heartache, happens to the righteous and unrighteous—*no one is exempt from grief or loss.* In our earthly human perspective, we try to reason good vs. bad, righteousness vs. unrighteousness, and fair vs. unfair. We attempt to balance an imaginary scale—we think our lives should include only good, right, and fair favor based on how we live our lives. We falsely believe that if we love and obey God, we will be spared any and every heartache. This simply is not true. Regardless of how we live our lives, grief happens to everyone—life simply is not fair at times.

John 10:10 says, *"The thief's purpose is to steal and kill and destroy. My purpose is to give them a rich and satisfying life."* (NLT) The enemy looks for ways to turn you against God and looks for areas of your life where he can steal, kill, and destroy. 1 Peter 5:8 says, *"Be alert and of sober mind. Your enemy the devil prowls around like a roaring lion looking for someone to devour."* (NIV) The enemy is ultimately the one to blame for stolen, killed, or destroyed life plans. God's desire is for each of us to have a rich and satisfying life. He wants to bless us with His goodness in our lives. Thanks to Adam and Eve—and the enemy bringing sin into their lives—we live in a fallen world. God gives every human being free will of choice and every human is fallible. When you have sin in the world, bad things happen as a result of that sin: loved ones die, marriages crumble, relationships falter, illness results, people mistreat others, all due to sin and a broken world. God gives definite blueprints in His Word, and if everyone followed God's ways, we'd live in a much better world. There are blessings and losses that all will go through in life, regardless if they deserve it or not. There simply are hard questions about life that might not ever have an answer until we have the opportunity to talk to God face to face. Some seriously unfair situations happen to people who do not deserve it. Even if an answer was given for why a heartbreaking situation happened, I do not believe it would offer relief from the pain. It sometimes is hard to submit to God's plans for our lives—and becomes even more difficult when bad things happen. The more heartbreaking the trial, the more we will struggle with ever accepting or understanding the situation. God truly understands that.

I wish that I could say that I submitted to God's purposes for the grief and loss He had allowed in my life early on, but unfortunately I did not. It took God many years of working on my heart and many years of brokenness before I allowed God access to my heart. Many wasted years of needless struggling passed before I finally submitted to God in the midst of my pain. *It took God allowing my heart to break—a break big enough so my hardened heart could crack to receive Him in—so that He could have access into my heart to change it.* If I could go back in time, I would have sought God and His heart much sooner. I would have cried out to Him, asking Him to give me wisdom, understanding, healing, and even joy in spite of my grievous circumstances. I truly believe I would have been better able to handle my sister's death had I submitted to God in the previous trials I went through before she died.

No one can control heartache or tragedy, but every single person can control whether they have God or His joy in their lives. I wish I would have understood the unique difference between happiness and joy. Happiness is dependent on our worldly circumstances—while joy is produced from an eternal perspective and relationship with God. As we grow closer to God, we understand that our present circumstances cannot compete with what He has in store for us in (and for) eternity. When we view our grief and circumstances through worldly eyes, we're left confused, frustrated, bitter, angry, anxious, and always in great pain. When we seek to see our circumstances through an eternal perspective, we find the ability to experience faith, love, comfort, peace, joy, and most importantly hope, regardless of our loss. Consider the following passages of scripture:

John 16:20-24, *"Very truly I tell you, you will weep and mourn while the world rejoices. You will grieve, but your grief will turn to joy. A woman giving birth to a child has pain because her time has come; but when her baby is born she forgets the anguish because of her joy that a child is born into the world. So with you: Now is your time of grief, but I will see you again and you will rejoice, and no one will take away your joy. In that day you will no longer ask me anything. Very truly I tell you, my Father will give you whatever you ask in my name. Until now you have not asked for anything in my name. Ask and you will receive, and your joy will be complete."* (NIV)

Isaiah 61:2-3, *"To proclaim the acceptable year of the LORD, and the day of vengeance of our God; to comfort all that mourn; To appoint unto them that mourn in Zion, to give unto them beauty for ashes, the oil of joy for mourning, the garment of praise for the spirit of heaviness; that they might be called trees of righteousness, the planting of the LORD, that he might be glorified."* (KJV)

When going through pain, it is always my goal to see my pain from God's perspective, to self-reflect, to see if there is anything I can learn from my situation, and to transition from being Grief-controlled into being God-guided throughout my grief process. For me, this is what has made the greatest difference in the outcome of how well I have fared a grief experience. When we seek to view our lives from God's perspective, He is faithful to remind us of His love for us—and that He has a plan and purpose for our lives. God plants life lessons into our hearts with each grief experience we face. As we allow Him to work through our trials, and heal our hearts, He is glorified. God knows each of us intricately, intimately, and fully. He not only knows each of us inside and out, He has actually engraved our names onto His hands. Isaiah 49:15-16 says, " *. . . I will not forget you! See, I have engraved you on the palms of my hands . . . "* (NIV) We are always on God's mind, *for He knows each of us by name.* God specifically makes a point to show us the depth of His love and concern for us. He could have simply engraved us onto one of His hands, but He makes the point to let us know that He has engraved us onto both palms.

Suffering and going through trials in life, although painful, is the ultimate way for God to mold us into being Christ-like—and He receives glory from that healing process. When you are wondering why God didn't prevent a heartache you have suffered, remember this: *God didn't even prevent His own Son, who lived a perfect blameless life, from suffering.* Jesus went through the grievous heartaches of loved ones dying, rejection, betrayal, temptation, being mocked and severely wronged, being gossiped and lied about, being cursed, brutally beaten, assaulted, and ultimately killed, among other life trials. Whatever you are going through, God feels your pain. He has gone through the same heartache and grief you are experiencing. Not only did He care enough to become human on earth, He resides in the heart of every believer—they are His adopted children, His very own creation. *Whatever tragedy a believer goes through, God goes through it as well since He lives inside their heart and He resides in their body, which is His holy temple.* 1 Corinthians 6:19-20, *"Do you not know that your body is the temple (the very sanctuary) of the Holy Spirit Who lives within you, Whom you have received [as a Gift] from God? You are not your own, You were bought with a price [purchased with a preciousness and paid for, made His own]. So then, honor God and bring glory to Him in your body."* (AMP) God paid a great price to have a relationship with you. He had the entirety of sin poured onto Him while on the cross and He willingly felt every detail of every sin as He suffered. He *can* relate to the pain you are going through.

Please understand that His heart breaks for you. Read this next passage of scripture and allow it to speak truth to your heart. When you go through suffering, you are sharing in God's suffering, and you will share in His glory too. *He will be making up for all of your pain.* He has not deserted or abandoned you. This next passage of scripture is long but well worth reading so you are able to *fully* grasp the truth of one of God's blueprints for suffering. So many people quote Romans 8:28 during times of grief, but to get the whole picture of God's heart and purpose for that verse, you need to look at the scriptures surrounding that often isolated verse to comprehend God's bigger picture. Although Romans 8:28 offers much hope, the surrounding verses offer a much greater portrait of hope. During your grief recovery, if a loved one offers you encouragement through the blessing of a specific verse, take time to read the entire chapter where the verse is found. I have found throughout my grief recovery that I am even more blessed when I seek to understand God's bigger picture for a verse through surrounding scriptures.

The truths found throughout Romans 8 are fundamental for understanding suffering—*"I consider that our present sufferings are not worth comparing with the glory that will be revealed in us . . . For the creation was subjected to frustration, not by its own choice, but by the will of the one who subjected it, in hope that the creation itself will be liberated from its bondage to decay and brought into the freedom and glory of the children of God. We know that the whole creation has been groaning as in the pains of childbirth right up to the present time. Not only so, but we ourselves, who have the firstfruits of the Spirit, groan inwardly as we wait eagerly for our adoption to sonship, the redemption of our bodies. For in this hope we were saved. But hope that is seen is no hope at all. Who hopes for what they already have? But if we hope for what we do not yet have, we wait for it patiently. In the same way, the Spirit helps us in our weakness. We do not know what we ought to pray for, but the Spirit himself intercedes for us through wordless groans. And he who searches our hearts knows the mind of the Spirit, because the Spirit intercedes for God's people in accordance with the will of God. **And we know that in all things God works for the good of those who love him, who have been called according to his purpose.** For those God foreknew he also predestined to be conformed to the image of his Son . . . If God is for us, who can be against us? He who did not spare his own Son, but gave him up for us all—how will he not also, along with him, graciously give us all things? Who will bring any charge against those whom God has chosen? It is God who justifies. Who then is the one who condemns? No one. Christ Jesus who died—more than that, who was raised to life—is at the right hand of God and is also interceding for us. Who shall separate us from the love of Christ? Shall trouble or hardship or persecution or famine or nakedness or danger or sword? . . . No, in all these things we are more than conquerors through him who loved us. For I am convinced that neither death nor life, neither angels nor demons, neither the present nor the future, nor any powers, neither height nor depth, nor anything else in all creation, will be able to separate us from the love of God that is in Christ Jesus our Lord."* (NIV)

I love the hope this passage of scripture offers! Our circumstances of suffering cannot compare to what God has planned for us—His glory that will be revealed in us. God tells us that one of the purposes for suffering is to refine us: to be liberated from our bondage to decay and brought into His freedom and glory. The Holy Spirit helps us in our weaknesses and intercedes for us continually, even in times when we do not have the words to know what we should ask for. The Spirit pleads and intercedes for us in accordance with God's perfect will for our lives. *If we love God,* He promises to work out His purpose for our lives—and everything we go through *will be* worked out for the ultimate good.

God loves each of us so much that He gave up His one and only Son, so that He could have a relationship with us. Our present circumstance did not catch God by surprise. He knew the hardships we would face, He knew we would need a relationship with Him throughout our joys and hardships in life, and He lovingly predetermined an *exact plan* of seeing us through our heartaches. We have an exclusive opportunity in times of heartaches and trials to be conformed into Christ's image—to go from being in bondage to the decay of this world to being brought into the freedom and glory that God freely offers us. There will come a day that God will graciously and abundantly give us *all* things. My favorite part of this verse is the truth that *NOTHING can separate us from Christ's love.* His love is not fickle, conditional, wavering, or limited. Christ's love is extravagant, unconditional, unending, with absolutely no bounds. His love has helped my heart to heal time and time again, conquering insurmountable mountains of grief. He makes us more than conquerors through Him *because of His great love!*

God loves people and desires to heal their pain. We may go through the fires of trials and grief, but after a period of time, He will return beauty for ashes, joy for mourning, and a garment of praise for the spirit of heaviness. Our grief will be turned to joy. In fact, we can experience joy even through the dark valleys we are walking through. Joy is not a feeling based on emotion, it is a hope that is based on God's promises. Joy is developed through delighting in God and His precepts, as well as taking refuge in Him, especially during trials.

Psalm 5:11, *"But let all who take refuge in you be glad; let them ever sing for joy. Spread your protection over them, that those who love your name may rejoice in you."* (NIV)

Psalm 19:8, *"The precepts of the LORD are right, giving joy to the heart. The commands of the LORD are radiant, giving light to the eyes."* (NIV)

I realize that you probably do not feel any joy at the moment. Joy was definitely not my first reaction to grief. Grief is hard, it is excruciatingly ruthless to the one experiencing the pain of loss, *but* there is hope if you will make the decision to trust God and run into His arms. I'm not saying that if you will only trust God during your times of grief that you will be skipping through fields of flowers, with a smile, while beautiful rainbows appear. I'm *not* suggesting that you'll have a joyfully blissful Pollyanna experience during your grief recovery. No, I'm not suggesting that at all. Grief is terribly painful and threatens to leave you a lifeless shell. I *am* saying that if you seek God, He is faithful to carry you when you are not able to handle the pain. He will walk alongside you throughout your entire grief process as you come to the place where you are able to truly live life and enjoy it once again.

I can't tell you a timeline of when you will have the ability to live life fully again, or how long your grief recovery will be, because everybody grieves very differently. I can tell you that in my multiple experiences with loss, *God has a unique timetable for grief each and every time.* He desires for grief, and the lessons He has for you, to not be rejected, wasted, or squandered. It sounds absurdly illogical but embrace your grief. Although intensely painful, it's ultimate purpose and life lesson is not meant to confuse, harm, or frustrate you. I know of several people who found that in some ways, loss is the very thing they needed to put life in perspective for their greater good.

As you embrace your grief, take time to get real with God and real with your self. Acknowledge your loss and choose to process your pain as best as you can. When you come to the place of genuinely getting real with God, your grief, and yourself . . . you then will have the ability to live a genuinely real life. As you gain a genuinely real and authentic life, you will experience a new authenticity in your relationship with God as well.

I imagine you may be bitter right now. I know I became bitter during times of grief, but I can tell you from experience that it will not help you to stay bitter at God or others. Bitterness harms only you as well as your loved ones around you. It is understandable to question why a trial has been allowed—it is a natural response to try to make sense of or understand why your world is crumbling around you. There are some trials and losses that I have been able to understand why I had to go through them, but to be honest, there are many that I will most likely never know or receive an answer on earth as to why I had to go through them. At those times, I choose to trust in God's sovereign power, wisdom, and goodness, and I choose to believe that God is in control. I choose to depend on God for His encouragement and love to carry me through. I know that He has a plan that my human mind could never comprehend and I choose to have faith that He knows what's best in accomplishing His ultimate goals and plans for my life.

Ephesians 2:10, *"For we are God's handiwork, created in Christ Jesus to do good works, which God prepared in advance for us to do."* (NIV) Everything we go through in life, and all the good we can do as a result of our trials, has been prepared in advance for us. We do not have to go through a trial with fear, anxiety, or confusion in our hearts. God *is* in control. As we seek His heart and submit to the plans He has for our lives, He takes over and guides us in accomplishing His purpose for every good or bad thing we go through. I have found that God is a safe refuge and secure shelter for the storms in life. Even though I wrestle with my questions, I can still feel His love and presence. I can trust in this: *God never allows His children to go through a difficult situation in vain.*

It is okay to feel what you need to feel, to ask God questions, or to *respectfully* vent to Him. Jesus respectfully questioned the Father twice during His last days on earth:

Matthew 26:39, *Going a little farther, he fell with his face to the ground and prayed, "My Father, if it is possible, may this cup be taken from me. Yet not as I will, but as you will."* (NIV)

Matthew 27:46, *About three in the afternoon Jesus cried out in a loud voice, "Eli, Eli, lema sabachthani?" (which means "My God, my God, why have you forsaken me?") . . . "* (NIV)

Throughout scripture, some questioned God as a way to seek to understand, like David did when he pleaded with God during his times of grief:

Psalm 42:9, *"I say to God my Rock, "Why have you forgotten me? Why must I go about mourning, oppressed by the enemy?"* (NIV)

Psalm 22:1-2, *"My God, my God, why have you forsaken me? Why are you so far from saving me, so far from my cries of anguish? My God, I cry out by day, but you do not answer, by night, but I find no rest."* (NIV)

God is not going to turn on you, or count it against you, if you respectfully question a loved one's death, a tragedy that happened, or if you question the reason for your pain. To question as a way of processing your pain is understandable. Sometimes, God will reveal an answer immediately. Sometimes, you will receive an answer at a later time. Other times, you may not receive an answer in this lifetime. God's will is difficult to understand at times. We have to remember that His ways are not our ways and His thoughts are not our thoughts. His intelligence and His plans have no bounds, unlike humans. His wisdom and purposes are far above what our earthly minds can ever wrap around to reason or comprehend. Isaiah 55:8 says, *"My thoughts are nothing like your thoughts," says the Lord. "And my ways are far beyond anything you could imagine."* (NLT)

Some grievances in life are due to death, some because of our own decisions, some the direct result of others, while some seem to have no rhyme or reason at all. To feel what you need to feel, to seek God for answers, or to respectfully vent to Him is part of the process of healing, but *do not become stuck in bitterness while seeking God.* Avoid it at all costs! Bitterness will continually drain you, leave you isolated, and compound your guilt in the days to come. Work out your grief in as honorable a way as you can.

I will caution you to seek God with the upmost respect and honor if you go to Him for answers. The Bible clearly warns us to not argue with God or go to Him in a quarreling spirit. Isaiah 45:9 says, *"What sorrow awaits those who argue with their Creator. Does a clay pot argue with its maker? Does the clay dispute with the one who shapes it, saying, 'Stop, you're doing it wrong! 'Does the pot exclaim, 'How clumsy can you be?'* (NLT) Another translation of the Bible says it is woeful for the one who quarrels with God. If you are tempted to blame God or quarrel with Him, take time to read the book of Job in the Bible. Job went through horrific loss, but never once turned against God or blamed Him. Job 1:21-22, *"He said, "I came naked from my mother's womb, and I will be naked when I leave. The Lord gave me what I had, and the Lord has taken it away. Praise the name of the Lord!" In all of this, Job did not sin by blaming God."* (NLT) God's Word tells us that it is a *sin* to blame God. Although Job's loss was horrific, he placed his complete trust in God—allowing God total access to work out His purposes through him during his time of grief. He praised God even while going through extreme grief and tragedy. Job and David are both excellent role models we can learn from during times of grief, trials, and heartache.

God created every single life. When He created each person while in the womb, He already knew the purposes for that life while they were being formed. He knew what each and every day was going to hold during the course of their life, and molded them to perfection for His ultimate plans—and their ultimate good. We will not always understand or agree with God's purpose, design, or plans, but He is the Potter and we are the clay. It is so important to realize this truth in the midst of tragic heartbreak and grief. To understand this principle, you will need to rely on God's grace. It is not something you can fully grasp—or accept—with a human mentality, because a human mind will desire to turn to bitterness, contention, and depression. God will help us find the grace we need to move forward into a peaceful and loving relationship with Him in the midst of our grief *if we run to Him.* We need to realize that He is the Author and we are the book. *You may be in the worst chapter of your life, but your life story isn't over yet.* Give the remaining chapters of your life to God, trusting Him to work out your life purpose for the ultimate good.

When you choose forgiveness, peace, comfort, mercy, and grace instead of bitterness, God is faithful to work His good out in your life. *He truly is able to make your life experience with Him greater than any experience with grief or loss you may face.* Pour your heart out to God, share with Him your struggles, your heartaches, your pain, any injustice that was done to you, and ask Him to begin the healing process. God is the only way I have found to truly heal my grieving heart. If you are concerned with sharing your thoughts, heart, or feelings with God . . . or you are considering running away from Him . . . consider the truths of Psalm 139:1-12, *"O Lord, you have examined my heart and know everything about me. You know when I sit down or stand up. You know my thoughts even when I'm far away. You see me when I travel and when I rest at home. You know everything I do. You know what I am going to say even before I say it, Lord. You go before me and follow me. You place your hand of blessing on my head. Such knowledge is too wonderful for me, too great for me to understand! I can never escape from your Spirit! I can never get away from your presence! If I go up to heaven, you are there; if I go down to the grave, you are there. If I ride the wings of the morning, if I dwell by the farthest oceans, even there your hand will guide me, and your strength will support me. I could ask the darkness to hide me and the light around me to become night—but even in darkness I cannot hide from you. To you the night shines as bright as day. Darkness and light are the same to you."* (NLT)

God already knows every intimate detail of your heart, mind, life, grief, thoughts, actions, and feelings. He knows the details of every happening in your life—*start to finish.* There is no possible way to hide from God . . . or avoid His presence, strength, love, or blessings. He knows what you are going to say, think, or feel before you even realize it—He is *that* in tune with you and concerned for you! In His great love, He created you—He knows you better than anyone could ever hope to know you—including yourself! Since God knows every detail about your life, heart, thoughts, actions, and feelings, you no longer need to be concerned about revealing these things to God. Take the time to pour your heart out to Him, share your thoughts and feelings with Him. No matter how hard you try, you simply cannot hide from His extravagant love and concern for you. Seek God with your whole heart during times of grief. He will fill you with His love and comfort in a way that only He is capable of. He has the ability to take you from the pain of being Grief-controlled over to the joy of being God-guided. God is the answer, throughout your grief, to finally get your breath back that life knocked out of you.

If you would like to have a relationship with God, and become His child, invite God into your heart. He then is faithful to give you a constant Comforter, His Holy Spirit. If you want to ask God to come into your heart and life, and to lead you throughout your grief experience, recovery, and life, you will want to pray a prayer such as this:

"Heavenly Father, I come to you and ask You to begin Your merciful process of healing my broken heart. Help me to transfer the way I view my grief and circumstances from a worldly and human perspective over to a Godly and eternal perspective. Help me to see that you have a plan for all circumstances, even if I am not able to see, understand, or accept that plan in the midst of my pain. Right now I ask You to come into my heart and to forgive me of all my sins. I believe that you died on a cross for me and conquered death. I give you my heart and ask You to make me Your child, and to guide and direct me throughout life. I give you each and every loss experience I am going through and I will trust you to work it out for my good. Open my heart and my eyes so that my experience with You is greater than any experience with grief or loss I may face. If I have hardened my heart, I ask You right now to take away my heart of stone and replace it with a soft heart that is moldable only by You. Help me to make the transition from being Grief-controlled into being God-guided. Fill my heart, life, spirit, and soul with You, Your Holy Spirit, and a joy that only You can give. Begin in me the true process of genuinely healing my heart. In Jesus name, Amen."

3 Oxygens

1. Invite God to lead you through your grief—ask Him to grant you wisdom, understanding, and grace and ask Him to drench you with His love, comfort, and mercy. Invite Him to walk closely beside you through your grief. Ask Him to reveal to you how to get your breath and life back.

2. Pour your heart out to God, share with Him your feelings, thoughts, struggles, heartaches, pain, any injustice that was

done to you, and ask Him to begin the healing process. Ask God to lead the way in guiding and directing your life and grief, and ask Him to make your paths straight.

3. Become a "student" of God. Read the Bible and see what God's Word has to say specifically to you. Study all about Him, find out what delights Him, obey Him, and honor Him with your life. Get to know God for yourself and form your own individual opinion about Him after reading His Word completely. Too many times, we allow others to guide our opinions and thoughts about God. You will have a new found ability to genuinely fall in love with God as you genuinely get to know Him yourself. Develop an individual authentic love relationship with God.

CHAPTER 3

~

The Oxygen of Encouragement

During times of grief, I have found that God truly encourages hurting hearts and often graciously provides others who have been through a similar experience to walk close beside us. God longs for each of us to go to Him with our hurt, pain, and suffering. He desires for us to go to Him during times of heartache, disappointment, and devastation, as well as during times of joy, blessings, and triumphs. He wants every part of our lives unconditionally with nothing held back. He desires to draw hurting hearts close to His own heart to show His encouraging power. After we fully submit to Him, we enter into the most beautiful relationship of encouragement. God is willing to allow whatever joy or heartache is necessary to achieve His perfect will in our lives—and He graciously supplies us with the mercy, grace, hope, and encouragement we need to fulfill His will for our lives on a daily basis. His perfect will is where you want to be. You will find a new hope for living and will feel energized when you are truly fulfilling His purpose and plans for your life.

The moment we begin to draw near to God's heart, loving Him with all of our heart, mind, soul, and strength, He is faithful to draw near to us, and shower us with comfort and encouragement through his Holy Spirit. God can and will use others to offer encouragement, but I have found that God is the ultimate Encourager.

People crave encouragement during their times of struggle and heartache, but sometimes family and friends do not know what to say—or even how to offer encouragement during times of grief. People can be so limited in their ability to encourage others, especially in comparison with God. We as humans usually look at the here and now, focusing on what our earthly eyes can see, but God is looking from a canvas of ages. He is our Creator and knows everything about us. He fully knows and understands our hearts—and He knows what His ultimate plans are for us on earth. His plans may look confusing to us, but from His viewpoint, He sees the entirety of our lives—*beginning to end.* He knows exactly what trials and encouragement we will need throughout our lives for our ultimate good.

Allow me to share an analogy with you that was inspired from a conversation I had with my mother about tapestries. Have you ever seen someone create a tapestry? If you look at the tapestry from the creator's point of vision, you can see the pattern, the brilliant colors, and you're able to clearly see, understand, and appreciate the beauty that the creator sees. If you were to look at the underside of the tapestry, it appears to be a jumbled up mess of dysfunctional colors and confusion. That's how life, grief, loss, and trials are. Our lives are God's tapestries and He is faithful to create in each of us a work of art for His purpose. To us, our lives and grief can appear to be a jumbled, ugly, confusing mess—but we aren't able to see the end result that God has planned for our lives. It is so important to remember that what is allowed to happen in our lives on earth is not only for earth itself, but is also preparation for what God has for us in Heaven for all eternity. We can trust God to work out His perfect plans for our lives . . . and to fill our lives with the circumstances and relationships that He deems best. God specifically grants us family and friends to "complete" every detail of the tapestries of our lives—and they complete us by offering encouragement to our hearts during times of grief. A relationship with God, as well as encouraging family and friends, is God's "thread" to hold the tapestry pieces of our lives together. If we are not able to presently see any beauty in our lives or circumstances, it simply means God can see the end result and He isn't finished with us yet. Philippians 1:6 says, *"And I am convinced and sure of this very thing, that He Who began a good work in you will continue until the day of Jesus Christ [right up to the time of His return], developing [that good work] and perfecting and bringing it to full completion in you."* (AMP) God began a good work in you and He is faithful to do whatever is needed to perfect and complete it. If you are seeking His heart, He will not allow your pain to be in vain . . . and He will not leave or quit on you.

Grief doesn't always make sense and there are horrible tragedies that happen in life that can never be understood or even accepted. Sometimes, people are not sure how to offer needed encouragement during those times. I have found that the more difficult the situation, the less people understand how to respond. Grief and loss makes others very uncomfortable unless they have been through a similar situation. When people hear about other's difficulties, it brings to their mind that they aren't exempt from a similar situation happening to them or their family. It's as though they feel like tragedies are contagious. You may find that the best encouragers will be family and friends who have been through a similar trial. You will also find that sometimes God wants to be your sole source of encouragement. After going through one specific trial, I noticed that a large portion of my friends were not a very big source of encouragement. After seeking God's heart in my discouragement, I could clearly see that He wanted to carry me through that difficult time, that He wanted to be the one to encourage me—so He unmistakably could receive the glory for getting me through that painful situation.

Very often, God will provide outside sources of encouragement. At other times, He wants to be your exclusive source of comfort and encouragement. It is understandable to be disappointed or frustrated in other's abilities to comfort you during your grief process, or to ask God why you are having to go through a fiery trial of grief by yourself. Please realize that not everyone is properly equipped to know how to minister to a grieving heart and there are some situations where you will fare better leaning exclusively on God. When you are at the end of your rope, when you feel extremely discouraged and downcast, when you feel hopeless, please understand that there will come a day where God will make all things right. One day there will be no more death, mourning, crying, or pain. God will wipe every tear and make all things new and right. It's hard to comprehend that truth in the middle of such heartbreaking pain, but God states His faithfulness in Revelation 21:4, *"God will wipe away every tear from their eyes; and death shall be no more, neither shall there be anguish (sorrow and mourning) nor grief nor pain any more, for the old conditions and the former order of things have passed away."* (AMP)

We need to remember during times of desperate heartache that we were created for God's purpose—and sometimes that purpose includes pain, loss, and grief. He *does* have a definite plan and purpose for every situation we go through in life—and He's very concerned we learn and apply what He is trying to reveal to us through times of grief and loss. What He has in store for us for the future (or the eternal) is much more important than our present day comfort or sufferings. Romans 8:18, *"I consider that our present sufferings are not worth comparing with the glory that will be revealed in us."* (NIV)

When going through trials and grief, many continue to struggle with the question, "why?" A few years ago, I certainly remember asking God "why" during a very trying time of constant pain and discouragement. I was desperate to try to understand the purpose for every loss that was compounding on top of one another without any respite. As I struggled in great pain, I cried out to God several times, but it seemed as though He didn't care about the circumstances I was going through. To go through one difficult circumstance after another for three straight years was draining, heartbreaking, and disheartening. It felt as though life would never get better, and I was left frustrated and discouraged from going through trial after trial after trial. I also was confused because God had previously helped me through my sister's death and other trials . . . so *why could I not feel His presence now?*

During these difficult three years:

- my grandmother died a few days before Christmas
- my son was diagnosed with facial tumors
- After several consultations and surgeries, my son was referred to two different hospitals (one in another city and the other in a different state)
- my son's close friend (who also was a family friend) died
- my favorite great-aunt and my husband's grandmother died on the same day
- I had a cancer scare that required surgery
- my marriage began to crumble almost to the point of divorce (God later healed and deepened our testimony as a result of this difficult time)
- my sister's second fiancé died unexpectedly on Easter
- my son's father died
- another close friend of my son died

- I had another cancer scare that required more surgery

I felt as though life was dunking my family and me in an ocean of grief and we barely had time to catch our breath before being dunked again. I know of people who have gone through far worse situations than what I just described, but to me all of this was painful, and I was left confused, broken, and hurt as to why God would allow all of this to take place in such a short amount of time. To go through seven deaths, multiple medical situations, as well as marital conflict was heartbreaking. I felt as though my family and I could barely catch our breath before another trial or loss would knock our breath right back out of us. It was difficult to see God's hand in many of these situations of loss.

I questioned a hundred times why my son, my family, and I were all having to go through so much at once. I had heard my entire life that God loves us, has a purpose, and cares about every detail of our lives, but this was hard to grasp in the middle of so much pain. It was difficult during these trials to encourage those around me, especially since I felt so discouraged myself, but I needed to make sure my son and my family was okay. I didn't want my son to see me crying all the time so I cried when no one else was around which usually was after everyone was asleep. I can't tell you the amount of times during my son's illness, the deaths, and other trials, that I would cry until my eyelids would swell and chafe. I was desperate to find God through my tears. I needed Him and needed to know that He truly cared. I needed to know that there was a purpose for all the pain. I was desperate for His encouragement . . . and to know that He had a plan. In desperation, I did another biblical study on grief and life challenges, looking up any passage of scripture that could help me to better understand God's principles on grief, trials, suffering, and death. The Bible, much to my surprise, had much to say about trials, suffering, death, and grief. I had already researched what God's Word said about grief, but this time it really came alive to me . . . especially Psalms. Psalms truly spoke to my heart due to having more loss and grief to be able to relate to. I found that God reveals specific purposes for grief in His Word, one of my favorites being 1 Peter 1:6-9, *"In all this you greatly rejoice, though now for a little while you may have had to suffer grief in all kinds of trials. These have come so that the proven genuineness of your faith—of greater worth than gold, which perishes even though refined by fire—may result in praise, glory and honor when Jesus*

Christ is revealed. Though you have not seen him, you love him; and even though you do not see him now, you believe in him and are filled with an inexpressible and glorious joy, for you are receiving the end result of your faith, the salvation of your souls." (NIV)

In my quest to find God and His encouragement during my trials, I was able to see that God is not a ruthless, aloof, or uncaring God that delights in controlling or hurting us. I found through researching His Word that He is rich with compassion and encouragement. He truly is concerned about the most minute details of our lives, grief, and pain . . . even when we can't feel His presence. He never leaves us or forsakes us and He takes great note of every pain we suffer and each tear that we cry. He has a purpose even when we can't see or sense a reason for what is going on in our lives. When loss doesn't make any sense at all, it may be for a future purpose. I have found that God allows some heartaches in life to prevent greater heartache in the future . . . and although we do not feel like it at the moment, it could be for our greater good or someone else's future greater good. I found through my grief that God truly is compassionate and God's nature will never betray the fruits of His Spirit—His heart is rich in love, joy, peace, forbearance, kindness, goodness, faithfulness, gentleness and self-control.

One particular verse that always stands out to me during times of grief is Psalm 56:8. When I first saw this verse, it literally jumped off the page, grabbed hold of my heart, and forever changed the way I viewed God, trials, and grief. This verse has become my favorite to meditate on when going through grief because the truth of God's love and compassion in Psalm 56:8 is unmistakable. Consider the following verses to understand the depth of God's compassion, encouragement, and concern for you:

Psalm 56:8, *"You've kept track of my every toss and turn through the sleepless nights, Each tear entered in your ledger, each ache written in your book."* (MSG) The pivotal truth of Psalm 56:8 shows that God is right there in times of heartbreak. He doesn't aloofly ignore or forget about our pain. God *is* there, even when you can't sense His presence.

Romans 8:26, *"And the Holy Spirit helps us in our weakness. For example, we don't know what God wants us to pray for. But the Holy*

Spirit prays for us with groanings that cannot be expressed in words." (NLT)

How beautiful, attention grabbing, and amazing are both of these encouraging verses? God cares so much about our pain that He keeps track of every toss and turn we make throughout a sleepless night, He records each heartache in His book, and enters each tear we cry in a ledger! I was so encouraged to know that God cared about my heart and grief to that great of detail because there were many sleepless nights I cried many tears. This verse really spoke to my heart. There were so many times during my grief that I wondered if God truly cared how deep my pain ran. I found throughout scripture that He has not abandoned anyone who is in deep grief or pain. Whether your grief is the result of a death, life challenge, another person's actions, or even your own actions, God truly cares. He loves and cares about people so much! He's crazy about you and wants to offer you His healing. If you are going through a death, He longs to encourage and comfort your broken heart so draw near to Him. If you are going through loss because of another person's actions, He sincerely cares about the wrongful affliction you are suffering. Realize that He is a God of mercy and love—but He is also a God of justice. He will not allow someone to hurt His own children and get away with it. It may seem that God is not dealing with a situation but He is *in His timing.*

Cry out to God and ask Him for help. He will hear you and will be faithful to encourage you. If you are going through a trial due to a personal foolish decision, don't give up on God or feel as though your sin has placed a permanent wall in between you and Him. He has the power to restore you. No matter the reason for your grief and pain, God cares about every facet of what you are going through. He feels and understands your pain. His Spirit is so concerned about you that He intercedes for you through groans that words cannot express! Get alone with God, pour your heart out to Him, and bask in His word, soaking Him in. Read His Word, it is one of God's greatest gifts to equip us throughout life, especially during times of sorrow and life challenges.

God delights in being our primary source of encouragement, but He also mercifully blesses the bereaved with a strong support system of family, friends, and church members. There are many grief counselors, grief recovery organizations, and programs available to encourage and support those going through grief. He also graciously gives those who have been through a similar loss, the wisdom and compassion to know how to help another through their circumstance of grief. I have found that although God places family, friends, organizations, and programs in our lives to offer encouragement through times of loss, He truly is the only one who is available *all of the time*, day or night. It is an incredible blessing to have the gift of talking to Him during a sleepless night, He's available ALL the time. When people seek and rely on God to be their ultimate encourager, something truly special happens. As they receive comfort and encouragement from God, He equips them with the ability to comfort and encourage others.

2 Corinthians 1:3-4, 8-9: *"Praise be to the God and Father of our Lord Jesus Christ, the Father of compassion and the God of all comfort, who comforts us in all our troubles, so that we can comfort those in any trouble with the comfort we ourselves receive from God . . . We were under great pressure, far beyond our ability to endure, so that we despaired of life itself. Indeed, we felt we had received the sentence of death. But this happened that we might not rely on ourselves but on God . . . "* (NIV)

God has equipped others with the gift of being able to encourage and minister to you since they have already been through a similar experience. We truly learn through grief that when we rely on ourselves, we are fallible. We must learn to rely on God. I can't say this strongly enough: *you do not have to go through your grief alone.* I wholeheartedly encourage you to seek God first, then as He leads you, seek out the help and encouragement you need from the resources He provides: family, friends, church, pastors, counselors, organizations, or professionals. There is no shame in receiving support or encouragement during times of grief or loss, and there are many churches, organizations, programs, and professionals available to offer the healing encouragement your heart desperately needs. A great place to start is to call a local Bible-believing church and ask for information or referrals. If you are not a member of a church, I highly recommend you find a Bible-based church to join. Many churches provide pastoral care, counseling, and grief recovery programs, such as GriefShare, to assist you through your grief. I personally have never experienced GriefShare, but a trusted family friend who works for this organization speaks very highly of it. I know of many who have greatly benefitted from GriefShare, so you may want to look up information on GriefShare, and attend their free programs that are offered through multiple churches. I plan on participating in GriefShare at my church due to it being spoken so well of from so many people.

When it comes to your personal grief recovery, don't ever quit. Understand that it is a process and it's very important to be patient. If one church, organization, program, or counselor isn't meeting your needs, or you feel as though you are no longer making progress in your grief recovery after a sufficient amount of time, seek out another that is better equipped to encourage you and meet your needs. Ask God for wisdom as you seek to find qualified resources to help you in your grief recovery efforts. Allow Him to guide and direct where He wants you to be.

If you decide to seek Christian counseling or pastoral care, have a list already made of the losses you have experienced, beginning with your very first experience with grief or loss you faced. This helps the counselor or pastor to understand how best to help you, and allows them an overall picture of your grief and the losses you have experienced in life. It is important to write down your losses because you don't want to make strides in your grief recovery only to be knocked down later on by dealing with a previous loss you hadn't dealt with. I truly believe my depression wouldn't have been so severe had I dealt with earlier losses that occurred before my sister's death. I also encourage you to talk to God, the Wonderful Counselor, and share what is paining your heart. Make it a daily habit to share your heart and life experiences with God first and foremost. One of the hardest things about my sister's death was that she was the one I called to talk to about everything. Once she died, even though I have other great family members and friends, I felt very lost and alone since she was who I confided in most. It's great to talk to family and friends about the joys and sorrows of life, but it's more important to share your joys and sorrows with God because unlike people, He will never die. He truly is the only one who can offer you a sustainable, longterm, lasting relationship that never ends.

After making a list of the losses and grief you have experienced, you may want to take the time to grieve for each event that took place. So many times in life, we neglect to thoroughly face and go through what has pained us. Sometimes, we won't deal with a loss out of fear that our loss will seem insignificant to others . . . or that our loss will not be validated. Sometimes, we don't allow ourselves to grieve a loss because we don't want to admit our loss. I thought for many years that grief recovery was only for those who had experienced a loved one dying. Grief recovery extends to any loss you have experienced in life. If it significantly hurt you, grief recovery is useful and appropriate.

Do not needlessly go through grief by yourself and don't attempt to ignore, hide, or shorten your grief. Do not attempt to alter it by keeping yourself busy or denying your loss took place. Before my sister died, not knowing how to deal with the losses I had previously experienced, I just tucked them away deep in my heart. After my sister died, all of the heartaches I had experienced finally caught up to me as I had not dealt with the pain from these earlier trials and losses. When all of my pain came to the surface at the time of my sister's death, I attempted to fix my own heart. After that didn't work, I went to a bookstore and bought several books on grief recovery but none of them relieved my grief. They left me feeling frustrated and like a failure. I couldn't even grieve the "right" way, or in the correct order, as outlined in the books. I finally found hope and encouragement through drawing close to God and my family. I also sought pastoral care and help from friends who had been through similar grief.

God truly shows His great compassion in providing us with so many grief recovery resources: God, family, trusted friends, church, pastors, counselors, professionals, support groups, grief recovery organizations and programs, grief recovery books, and grief recovery centers. God blesses people with so many options to receive the encouragement, support, and help that is needed during times of loss, and there is no shame in obtaining help. *Getting the help, encouragement, and support you need helps you to eventually have the ability to love and enjoy life once again.*

Grief is so very complex in that the one going through grief isn't just experiencing their loss, they must also deal with all of the feelings associated with their loss that leaves them discouraged. To truly be able to allow encouragement to stay in, you need to get all feelings of discouragement out. Some of the most destructive feelings during times of grief are guilt and regret. Guilt and regrets are like being thrown in the middle of the ocean, slowly drowning in a sea of "what ifs" and "if onlys" while gasping for air. The unknown territory of grief is cruel, giving no one a compass to know how to get back to shore. During your most stressful and discouraging feelings, cry out to the only One who has the ability to bring you back to shore and heal your grief. Pause right now and ask God to bring encouragement into your life.

Dealing with guilt and regrets will leave you in a constant state of discouragement. When we understand that God has an ultimate plan, and works everything out for our good, we begin to realize our need to lay our grief, guilt, and regrets in His hands. Matthew 11:28-29, *"Come to me, all you who are weary and burdened, and I will give you rest. Take my yoke upon you and learn from me, for I am gentle and humble in heart, and you will find rest for your souls."* (NIV)

Something that helped me to overcome my guilt and regrets was making a list. Make a list of your guilts and regrets, then give each of your guilts and regrets over to God. If you have done something wrong, ask God for His forgiveness and grace. If you had wronged your loved one that passed away, ask them for their forgiveness through God. You may even want to write your deceased loved one a letter. If you have wronged a living person, or there is conflict as the result of your loss, ask for their forgiveness. They may or may not forgive you, *but God will*—and God rewards the humble. You may also need to forgive yourself.

After you have thoroughly gone through your list of losses, guilt and regret lists, or if you have written letters, consider shredding or tearing them up if you do not want for others to read them. After you have properly gone through your lists by yourself, with a pastor, or a counselor, it is not productive or conducive to keep any remembrance of them. When we work through our guilt and regrets, we then need to forgive ourselves. We truly need to pattern our forgiveness for ourselves after God's own heart. After we reflect and do these exercises, asking God for His forgiveness . . . we need to forgive ourselves. We then are truly able to leave it in God's hands.

2 Chronicles 7:14, *"if my people, who are called by my name, will humble themselves and pray and seek my face and turn from their*

wicked ways, then I will hear from heaven, and I will forgive their sin and will heal their land." (NIV)

Psalms 103:11-13, *"For as high as the heavens are above the earth, so great is his love for those who fear him; as far as the east is from the west, so far has he removed our transgressions from us. As a father has compassion on his children, so the LORD has compassion on those who fear him"* (NIV)

Seeking God, I learned a brand new perspective on every trial I had been through. God showed me the way to: effectively deal with guilt and regrets, to heal my broken heart and spirit, to help me have the ability to live again, and to not merely go through the depressed motions of living or simply put on a "happy face" for the benefit of others. God taught me how to have true joy in spite of my grief and circumstances. I felt as though God was tugging at my heart and saying, "You have two choices of how to handle your grief: *your* way or *My* way. Choose *My* encouragement, choose *Me.*"

Everybody has two choices after any loss they may experience: choose to live the remainder of life in a lifeless, hopeless, depressed, miserable existence . . . or create a new life that is filled with renewed hope, encouragement, and purpose. After loss occurs, each person has the ability to regain their breath back, and possibly even achieve a life that is better than the one they are currently living. It will not be the life they once had, for life can never be like it was before a loss takes place . . . *but* . . . each person can allow God to create a life that not only gets them through the day, but a life where they feel fulfilled, encouraged, and even experience deep joy.

You have a decision to make right now: do you want to allow God to perfect His ultimate purpose for your life or do you want to allow your grief to overtake your heart and life? Nobody can make this decision for you, you will have to decide for yourself. Do you want to make the decision to take hold of your grief, embrace the pain, seek God's encouragement, and come out of your heartbreaking ordeal better . . . *or* . . . do you want to become so immersed in your pain that you drown in the oceans of your grief, miss out on future opportunities, squander memories with loved ones, and reject what God has in store for you? I hope you will decide to take a deep breath with God's help, and embrace His encouragement and purpose for your grief, for God custom designed your life and healing process uniquely for you. It's His desire to help you through your pain, to make something beautiful out of something that the enemy meant to harm you. Don't allow the enemy, or anybody else, the opportunity to destroy your life any further. Seek God and ask Him to make beauty from ashes. Read God's Word, especially the books of Job, Psalms, and Proverbs, and find God's way through your grief. This is your opportunity to be led through your grief by God Himself. He is faithful to fill you with encouragement and hope—and encouragement and hope are what you most need to overcome your struggles through grief. God, through His amazing hope and encouragement, will eventually help you to find the way out of your pain.

Romans 5:3-5, *"And not only that, but we also glory in tribulations, knowing that tribulation produces perseverance; and perseverance, character; and character, hope. Now hope does not disappoint, because the love of God has been poured out in our hearts by the Holy Spirit who was given to us."* (NKJV)

2 Thessalonians 2:16-17, *"May our Lord Jesus Christ himself and God our Father, who loved us and by his grace gave us eternal encouragement and good hope, encourage your hearts and strengthen you in every good deed and word."* (NIV)

"Lord, Thank you so very much for Your love and for making Yourself available to talk to and encourage me every second of every day. Thank you for your Word and for the people, organizations, professionals, and resources You have supplied me with to help encourage me through my times of grief. It is so good to know that I am never alone throughout my grief for You are at my right hand and nothing can shake me. Lord, please bring encouragement, hope, and true healing to my heart, and cover me with Your perfect love, grace, and mercy. When I feel at my lowest, rescue me from discouragement. When I feel like quitting, lift me up so that I can seek You. As I seek You, shower me with encouragement and graciously supply me with the encouraging resources I need to heal. Reveal Your truths and Your love to my heart. I love You and thank You, Lord. In Jesus Name I pray, Amen."

3 Oxygens

1. Seek the encouragement you need through God and His Word, family, friends, pastors, counselors, grief recovery organizations and programs, professionals, and grief centers.

2. Create a list of your losses, a guilt and regret list, and consider writing a letter to your deceased loved one. Be sure to guard these lists and tear them up if you do not want others to read them. After you have properly gone through these list exercises with God, by yourself, with a pastor, or a counselor, shred them. Place your grief, discouragement, regrets, and guilt in God's hands, forgive yourself, and let it go.

3. Do a Bible study on grief, trials, suffering, and death and see what God reveals to your heart.

CHAPTER 4

~

The Oxygen of Gratefulness, Thankfulness, and Praise

God has blessed every believer with a life melody. Often times, when going through grief, the melody in one's heart is lost. As we submit to God throughout our grief, He helps us to find the individual melody He has placed in our heart once again in spite of loss. God desires for our hearts to praise Him through the storms we go through in life. To thank Him for all of the blessings He has bestowed on us throughout our lives is a powerful antidote to a grieving heart. For our grief recovery to be most effective, it is vital to find the songs in your heart of gratefulness, thankfulness, and praise to God.

God is our deliverer. When we turn to Him with genuine love and praise, He is faithful to fulfill His ultimate plans for our grief and lives. As we take refuge in God, making Him our song of Love, He becomes our strength and a mighty fortress. Psalm 59:16, *"But I will sing of your strength, in the morning I will sing of your love; for you are my fortress, my refuge in times of trouble."* (NIV)

Thank God for what He has done throughout your life, for the times He has delivered you, and thank Him for all that He is planning to do. He is the only One who has the power to turn wailing into dancing by turning your grief into joy. He does this so that your heart can be awakened to sing Him a new song of thankfulness forever. Psalm 30:11-12, *"You turned my wailing into dancing; you removed my sackcloth and clothed me with joy, that my heart may sing to you and not be silent. O Lord my God, I will give you thanks forever."* (NIV)

The experience of God putting a new song in your heart during times of grief is unmistakeable. You begin to see the beauty in even the smallest things, becoming truly thankful and grateful for all of the blessings you receive. Psalm 13:6 says, *"I will sing to the LORD, for he has been good to me."* (NIV)

I truly believe that nothing develops true gratefulness and genuine praise more than loss. When loss occurs, we distinctly see all that we had before a loss took place. It is also during our times of loss that we are able to precisely and purely see all that God continually blesses us with on a daily basis. When we view our grief through an eternal viewpoint, we develop a strong sense of thankfulness for all of the good He allows in our lives—especially during times of tragedy. God is good all of the time . . . not just *some* of the time . . . but *all* of the time. *The only reason anyone has the gifts and blessings they enjoy in life is because of Him.* All of the good in your life, from birth to present, is because He willed it so. The family and friends that you have enjoyed thus far in your lifetime, it is because He created them and allowed them to be a part of your life. God graciously allows us to borrow loved ones for a time. Family, children, spouses, and friends are all gifts and blessings sent straight from God. It is not up to us when these gifts are given to us by Him—or when we must return these borrowed gifts.

My parents have been amazing examples of trusting God and showing gratefulness in action, even during grief. Throughout my childhood and life, they have made it known how grateful they are for the gifts of God, family, relationships, and blessings. At my sister's funeral, my mom did something that truly inspired me to view my blessings from God through an eternal perspective. At the end of the service, my mom got up in front of hundreds of people who attended my sister's funeral and thanked God for allowing her the privilege of being my sister's mom for 22 years. My mom is a bright testimony of loving God and being thankful to Him, even through heartbreaking situations of loss. When my siblings and I were born, my mom dedicated each of us to God at a baby dedication service at church. To express gratefulness to God for the time He entrusted my sister to her care, my mom chose to publicly thank God for my sister's life and publicly released her back to God's care after He called my sister Home. What a beautiful way to publicly show gratefulness to God while praising Him for His goodness! My

Public thanking God loved one & release him to God 44

mom also read the poem, A Child Loaned by Edgar A. Guest, right after she released my sister back to God. I have included this beautiful poem at the back of this book.

In 1 Thessalonians 5:18-19, we are given instructions to *"Thank God in everything [no matter what the circumstances may be, be thankful and give thanks], for this is the will of God for you [who are] in Christ Jesus [the Revealer and Mediator of that will]. Do not quench (suppress or subdue) the [Holy] Spirit."* (AMP) When we go through challenging situations of grief, we are given an opportunity to draw others to Christ's heart. There is something remarkable when a person goes through a difficult situation and they trust and praise God. It is even more impressive when a person going through grief has a lifestyle of genuine thankfulness. No one is going to be thankful for a loved one's death, but we still have the ability to be thankful for God's remaining goodness in our lives. I think it is interesting that after God instructs us to be thankful in every situation, He gives the additional instruction to not suppress the Holy Spirit. How do we obey the instruction to not suppress God's Spirit? By allowing God to work through every situation we face in life so that He receives the glory for getting us through our trials, and by allowing His Holy Spirit to instruct, comfort, and love us. Never suppress what His Spirit can accomplish through your life . . . especially through your grief. If you feel as though you do not have the strength to go on, tell Him that—seek His heart and His help. Open up and share your entire heart and life with Him. When you trust God through hardships, and allow Him to develop a deep thankfulness in your heart, a testimony is in the making. God will create and develop a beautiful testimony in a thankful heart that is sold-out in love with Him.

So many times in life and loss, we become angry at God because we lack an eternal perspective. We fail to properly view God and we lack a spirit of genuine gratefulness, thankfulness, and praise. I once went to a conference where the speaker gave an unforgettable analogy. The analogy explained that if a person came to your door and blessed you with a $100 bill every single day for years, would you become angry or bitter with the person if they suddenly stopped blessing you with the daily unwarranted $100 bill. Loved ones are the same principle, in that God blesses us with loved ones daily. We have done nothing to warrant the rich blessing of loved ones—they all are unmerited as we have done nothing to deserve them. God blesses and rewards us with the beautiful gift of relationships, regardless of our behavior, and we do not have to work for it. When God decides to take His borrowed creation back, it truly is excruciatingly painful. *We must come to terms with the fact that our loved ones ultimately belong to God and not us.* We are simply borrowing our loved ones for awhile until God is ready to call them Home. I'm not saying that it is easy to have an eternal perspective at all times, because it is not. It was difficult to develop an eternal perspective when my dad, sister, and other loved ones died, and it was difficult to understand why God chose to call them Home at such a young age. I wasn't ready for them to die, and it was frustrating not being able to sense a reason for their deaths. I had to make a daily decision to focus on the eternal perspective of my grief or I would have become completely discouraged. We need to continually develop an eternal perspective each and every day so that we will be in tune with God's heart and His purpose for our lives. We have two choices we can make after a loved one dies: we can focus on being angry that our loved one has been taken from us or we can focus on being grateful for the time we were allowed to be a part of their life. We can praise God for the fact that He thought so highly of us that He blessed us with our loved ones and we can be grateful for the time we had with them.

It is totally okay to initially be angry for awhile, that is a normal part of grieving—but we must not stay stuck in our anger because it will eventually turn into bitterness. If we give into bitterness, it will eventually control every aspect of our lives, and change who we are as a person, so guarding our hearts is of great importance. Proverbs 4:23, *"Guard your heart above all else, for it determines the course of your life."* (NLT) It is perfectly okay to continue to love and miss loved ones, and it is okay to wish they were still here, *but* our hearts need to make the transition from being angry or bitter into praising and thanking God for the time we had with our loved ones while they were with us.

It is vital to choose thankfulness, gratefulness, and praise instead of bitterness. If you look at a rose, it has beauty as well as thorns. Grief is truly like a rose: I believe that we are able to escape the thorns of bitterness as we focus on the sweet fragrance and beautiful petals of the rose instead. What we focus on while going through the heartache of grief will direct our hearts and lives. If we primarily focus on nothing but our loss, we will live a life of loss. If we focus on being grateful, we will live a life of gratefulness which opens our eyes to the remaining beauty in our lives. It is very important to be grateful for the family, friends, and blessings that God still blesses us with. Imagine picking up a rose and pricking your finger on the thorns. If you were to focus on the pain in your finger, you would never see the beauty of the rose. What if there was an entire rose garden that you would never be able to see because of the pain? It is so easy to focus on our pain and loss to the point of forgetting to focus on the blessings we still have in life—and the future blessings we may receive.

Every loss is an opportunity to develop gratefulness, thankfulness, and praise in our lives so *we are able to live life more fully and purposefully.* Losing a loved one is never easy . . . it will take time and effort to develop thankfulness, gratefulness, and praise into our lives during times of heartache. If it were an easy task, everyone would go around with a huge smile on their face at all times, even in the middle of grief. No, it probably will not be easy developing these character traits during times of great heartache. As we ask God for His grace and help, He will be faithful to teach us the qualities of thankfulness and gratefulness through the midst of our pain.

Throughout life, all we have is simply because of God's mercy. If we look at life through the lens of our present loss and grief, we will never praise God. We will eventually become stuck in our grief and fail to see all of the good that is still remaining in our lives.

Job had a mature and wise perspective on grief—Job 1:21, *"And said, Naked (without possessions) came I [into this world] from my mother's womb, and naked (without possessions) shall I depart. The Lord gave and the Lord has taken away; blessed (praised and magnified in worship) be the name of the Lord!"* (AMP) Job wisely understood that he was born with nothing and he will die with nothing. What is interesting about this verse is that Job had the ability to make this statement immediately after being told horrible news—the news that all ten of his children had died and he had lost all of his earthly wealth. Job was so in tune with the heart of God that he trusted God and God's plan fully, even when he didn't understand. What mattered most to Job was his relationship with God and praising Him. Our goal for life is not our life on earth or earthly things, for all of those things pass. Our goal is an exceptional relationship with God and heavenly things, because these things can never be taken away. Matthew 6:19-21 says, *"Don't hoard treasure down here where it gets eaten by moths and corroded by rust or—worse!—stolen by burglars. Stockpile treasure in heaven, where it's safe from moth and rust and burglars. It's obvious, isn't it? The place where your treasure is, is the place you will most want to be, and end up being."* (MSG) Whatever you decide to make your heart's treasure will ultimately lead your heart. When we make God and eternal treasures our priority, God will lead, guide, and direct our hearts. God is the source of all joy and every good thing. He will restore our hearts to where we can truly praise Him.

When we are tempted to think that we have gained good gifts in our lives all by ourselves, we need to consider James 1:17-18: *"Whatever is good and perfect comes down to us from God our Father, who created all the lights in the heavens. He never changes or casts a shifting shadow. He chose to give birth to us by giving us his true word. And we, out of all creation, became his prized possession."* (NLT) God is the only reason we have any good in our lives. He loves us so much that He not only gives us great gifts, He gave us first place among all creation. He could have chosen to have an exclusive relationship with animals or nature but He didn't—*He chose us.* He wanted to have a relationship with each of us. That is beyond comprehension to me. He also created us not just for here on earth, but for eternity as well. He wants to have a lasting relationship with us. If all of our relationships died here on earth, a permanent frustration would form, *but* our relationships do not have to die here on earth. God is so good that we will again enjoy a relationship with our loved ones once we are all in Heaven, if we have all trusted in Him and accepted Him. That is a truth to be grateful and thankful for. I praise God that He is going to allow me to eventually have a new improved relationship with my loved ones that now live in eternity. When my loved ones died, it was not *"Goodbye,"* it was *"I'll see you later."* How can I not be totally thankful for such an amazing gift like that? God could have chosen for relationships to permanently die and end, but in His great compassion, His plan included eternity. We can praise and thank God for His plans, and His design for relationships and eternity. Even more important to be praised is that His love is ours forever. 1 Chronicles 16:34, *"Give thanks to the LORD, for he is good;*

his love endures forever." (NLT) If we accept Him, we will one day go to live with Him for all eternity, and enjoy His love as well as a continual relationship with Him forever.

John 14:1-4 says, *"Don't let your hearts be troubled. Trust in God, and trust also in me. There is more than enough room in my Father's home. If this were not so, would I have told you that I am going to prepare a place for you? When everything is ready, I will come and get you, so that you will always be with me where I am. And you know the way to where I am going."* (NLT) How amazing is that? God is actively preparing a place for all who accept Him. The very moment he prepares the last detail of our Heavenly Home, He comes to get us. The way to get to where He resides (Heaven) is simple: John 14:6, *"Jesus said to him, I am the Way and the Truth and the Life; no one comes to the Father except by (through) Me."* (AMP) When we genuinely ask Jesus to live in our hearts, and truly accept Him, He makes us His child. He prepares a place for us in Heaven. (If you haven't trusted Jesus as your savior yet, there is a prayer you can pray at the end of Chapter 2).

As we deepen our relationship with God during our times of grief, making Him our highest treasure, a beautiful thing begins to transpire: *we begin to build our lives on Him and the truths of His Word instead of building our lives on grief.* As He begins to strengthen our faith through His Word, our hearts are filled with a thankfulness that overflows. Our faith begins to take a deep root into the heart of God, and through that deep root, we begin to appreciate God more and more. Colossians 2:7, *"Let your roots grow down into him, and let your lives be built on him. Then your faith will grow strong in the truth you were taught, and you will overflow with thankfulness"* (NLT) Having a deep relationship with God is the most rewarding treasure you can hope to have on earth. As we seek Him through prayer, reading His Word, and loving Him, we have the privilege of growing a rich and rewarding friendship with Him. As we grow in a love relationship with Him and delight in Him, He will give us the desires of our heart and stabilize our lives. Psalm 37:4, 23 says, *"Take delight in the Lord, and he will give you your heart's desires . . . The Lord directs the steps of the godly. He delights in every detail of their lives."* (NLT) When going through grief, our lives can seem unstable and confusing. As we make delighting in God our top priority, we find that He is more than faithful to guide and direct our steps. He balances our lives as we praise Him through life's storms. Psalm 34 does not suggest that God will give us every whim we ask of Him, for He is not a genie. As we delight in God, He changes and transforms our hearts to desire the same things His heart desires. *Our goal is not to change God to make Him be in sync with our wishes and desires—our goal is to allow Him to change us so that our wishes and desires are in sync with Him.*

Delighting in God is an amazing experience of sheer love. There is nothing like it on earth. As we purposefully make time to spend with God each day, He meets us exactly where we are. When we delight in God, He becomes our truest friend, a trusted confidant. He never leaves or quits on us as we pursue a relationship with Him. He will not falter or fizzle out on us. He is trustworthy, dependable, and stable—a true rock. We can freely pour our hearts out to Him and tell Him anything and everything. As we read His Word, scripture takes on a whole new meaning and begins to speak directly to our hearts. He faithfully pours His comfort and guidance into our hearts during daily quiet times with Him. He lovingly strengthens our hearts with each decision we make to become more like Him. Our love begins to take deep root as we choose to love, honor, adore, obey, and worship Him through all seasons of life. The harsh sting of grief is softened as we allow His Holy Spirit to truly minister to our hearts. There is no greater reward or treasure during times of grief than to have the priceless privilege of building a deep, illimitable friendship with God. A beautiful passage of scripture that sums up what a love relationship with God is all about is Psalm 86:8-17, *"There's no one quite like you among the gods, O Lord, and nothing to compare with your works. All the nations you made are on their way, ready to give honor to you, O Lord, ready to put your beauty on display, parading your greatness, And the great things you do— God, you're the one, there's no one but you! Train me, God, to walk straight; then I'll follow your true path. Put me together, one heart and mind; then, undivided, I'll worship in joyful fear. From the bottom of my heart I thank you, dear Lord; I've never kept secret what you're up to. You've always been great toward me—what love! You snatched me from the brink of disaster! . . . But you, O God, are both tender and kind, not easily angered, immense in love, and you never, never quit. So look me in the eye and show kindness, give your servant the strength to go on, save your dear, dear child! Make a show of how much you love me . . . As you, God, gently and powerfully put me back on my feet."* (MSG)

God is amazing and brings a deep healing to hurting hearts. Make time today to meet with Him and begin pouring your heart out to Him. Talk to Him about everything that is going on in your life, share with Him your pain, and tell Him about all that is troubling you. He is genuinely concerned for you and cares about your life in great detail. Again, if you're frustrated with Him, tell Him. He knows your heart, your thoughts, and every single facet about you and your life. He knows your past, but more importantly, *He knows the plans He has in store for your future.*

Meditate on the beautiful truths of Jeremiah 29:11-14: *"For I know the plans I have for you," declares the LORD, "plans to prosper you and not to harm you, plans to give you hope and a future. Then you will call on me and come and pray to me, and I will listen to you. You will seek me and find me when you seek me with all your heart. I will be found by you," declares the LORD, "and will bring you back from captivity."* (NIV) Even though you presently feel the piercing sting of grief, God still has a plan for your life. He wants to fill your life with hope and a future. God desires for you to call on Him and pray—building a solid relationship with Him while you seek Him with all your heart. He wants you to have a full life and the ability to enjoy it once again.

As you begin to build and deepen your relationship with God, don't be surprised if you are met with discouragement from the enemy. Make prayer, reading God's Word, and developing a heart of thankfulness, gratefulness, and praise top priorities while going through your experience with grief. Colossians 4:2, *"Devote yourselves to prayer with an alert mind and a thankful heart."* (NLT) Find out and know what God has to say in His Word. The more grounded we are in truth, the less likely we will fall to deception or lies. The enemy will attempt to take away any healing God blesses us with. He will try to discourage us and attempt to feed our minds with untruths during our grief recovery. It is imperative that we put on the whole armor that God provides us with *(Truth, righteousness, peace, faith, and salvation)* as we seek Him daily. With a thankful heart, praise Him for all He is accomplishing in your life. Ephesians 6:14-18 instructs us how to protect our hearts during times of trials: *"Be prepared. You're up against far more than you can handle on your own. Take all the help you can get, every weapon God has issued, so that when it's all over but the shouting you'll still be on your feet. Truth, righteousness, peace, faith, and salvation are more than words. Learn how to apply them. You'll need them throughout your life. God's Word is an indispensable weapon. In the same way, prayer is essential in this ongoing warfare. Pray hard and long. Pray for your brothers and sisters. Keep your eyes open. Keep each other's spirits up so that no one falls behind or drops out.*" (MSG)

Seek truth, righteousness, peace, and faith during your grief. Learn to build and apply these character traits into your daily life while embracing your salvation. Pray, read God's Word, and praise God continually. Encourage your brothers and sisters in Christ so that they feel uplifted. This is God's desire for every believer. God desires to fill our hearts up to a most full and rich level through Him. He mercifully grants us, and those around us, with the wisdom He extravagantly gives so that we are able to teach and counsel each other with the truths He supplies us with through His Word. He reveals His purpose and plans to us as we obey the truth of Colossians 3:16, *"Let the message about Christ, in all its richness, fill your lives. Teach and counsel each other with all the wisdom he gives. Sing psalms and hymns and spiritual songs to God with thankful hearts."* (NLT)

How do we develop thankfulness, gratefulness, and praise? We begin to develop these character traits by asking God to bless us with these traits. As we cooperate with God in developing thankfulness, gratefulness, and praise, we are able to praise God with thankful hearts, as we take the time to realize and see His mercy, grace, and goodness in our lives. Look for God in ALL things.

There are many ways to develop thankfulness to God. One of my favorite ways is by thanking God for all of the good He allows in my life. Take time today to do a complete inventory of every good thing in your life, then thank God for everything on your list. In your list, include God, people, jobs, spiritual blessings, necessities, material possessions, health, abilities, talents, attributes, provisions, programs, organizations, memories, favor, and anything else God brings to mind. Be as specific as you possibly can. As we truly appreciate God's blessings in our lives, we will develop grateful hearts that thank and praise God in every situation. We may not be thankful for our loss, *but* we can be grateful for the good remaining in our lives, and the lessons we learn throughout our grief process. We can also be grateful for all of the blessings God entrusts to us in spite of our grief.

A great way of developing gratefulness is to think of all of the people who have benefitted your life. Sit down and write thank you notes to every person who has significantly loved you, encouraged you, or who has poured blessings into your life. When I took the time to write notes of gratefulness, I also wrote to anyone who had helped me in life, or who had made a positive impact in my life. I wrote to my family, my past teachers who had educated me, former and present friends, employers, my sunday school teachers, and anyone else that had benefitted my life. To my surprise, I received several letters back, and I was amazed how much God blessed and healed my heart as I made thankfulness, gratefulness, and praise priorities in my life. Something else I did that was significantly healing to me was I wrote letters to my loved ones that had died. In my notes, I thanked them for all of the memories we had shared. I thanked them for what they meant to me. I asked for forgiveness for anytime I had not treasured them while I still had them in my life. I told them how important they were to me. After I wrote my letters to them, I placed the letters into an envelope and tucked them into my Bible.

Another way that you can build thankfulness, gratefulness, and praise into your life is by making your Bible an interactive personal experience with God. The Bible was important to me while growing up because my parents would read it to us. My Bible became of greater importance to me as I searched for God's heart while going through grief. My Bible is very interactive as I have underlined and highlighted all that God has shown me throughout my relationship with Him. My current Bible that I use was given to me by my parents after my son was born. When my son was a baby, God impressed on my heart to read His Word thoroughly and make my Bible into a legacy to give to my son as an adult. All of the treasures I have gleaned from God are underlined, highlighted, and I have filled the outward margins with truths God has shared with me throughout the last 20 years. I also have written prayer requests in my Bible and wrote the date that God answered. There were many times throughout a grief process that I was reminded of God's love and faithfulness as I opened my Bible and could see God's and my life journey together. As I opened

write notes to people who blessed me.

God's Word in times of discouragement, I praised Him for all of the trials He has carried me and my family through. I look forward to giving my Bible to my son on his wedding day. He will always have with him an interactive legacy of God's love as well as mine.

One of the best ways to develop praise is through praising God through music and song. Music truly is one of God's greatest gifts to us. Through music, we are able to unite our very spirit to God's heart. Praising and worshipping God turns our focus away from our grief and directs our spirit, heart, and eyes towards God. As we praise God through the storms in life, we begin to see our problems from an eternal perspective. Our problems do not magically go away, instead God begins to work through our grief as we praise Him and delight in Him. As we choose to praise God and run to Him in times of hardships, God transforms our hearts and infuses us with His peace. Peace is a direct benefit of praise—our heartache, worry, grief, and burdens are lifted when we go to God in praise. Matthew 11:28, *"Come to me, all you who are weary and burdened, and I will give you rest."* (NIV) There is such an unexplainable freedom in worshipping and praising God. It is in praising Him that I feel closest to His heart. When I sing praise songs to His heart, I truly connect with my beautiful Creator.

I love the creativity that God offers through music. I truly marvel how every song was created by a few fundamental notes—there are not many keys on a piano, yet there are thousands upon thousands of songs created by the musical notes God created. Music is emotionally powerful and there is a music genre for every mood and feeling that we will ever experience on earth. Music has the ability to put emotions into words and has the power to inspire.

One of the most beautiful types of music is hymns. Hymns have some of the most amazing stories of triumph over loss that you will ever hear. Studying hymns and reading about the songwriter's motivation for writing the hymns is a phenomenal study. One of my favorite hymns was written by Horatio Spafford. He wrote the beloved hymn, It Is Well With My Soul. What's remarkable and amazing about this hymn is that Horatio Spafford wrote it while going through major grief and loss. Within a few years time, Mr. Spafford lost majority of his earthly wealth in The Great Fire of Chicago, all four of his daughters died in a tragic drowning accident, and he had a young son die all within a short time. To go through crushing and unbearable grief . . . *and still praise God* . . . is beyond human explanation or comprehension. Take a moment and soak up the words from this amazing hymn:

When peace like a river, attendeth my way, When sorrows like sea billows roll;

Whatever my lot, Thou hast taught me to say, It is well, it is well, with my soul.

It is well, with my soul, It is well, with my soul, It is well, it is well, with my soul.

Though Satan should buffet, though trials should come, Let this blest assurance control,

That Christ has regarded my helpless estate, And hath shed His own blood for my soul.

My sin, oh, the bliss of this glorious thought! My sin, not in part but the whole,

Is nailed to the cross, and I bear it no more, Praise the Lord, praise the Lord, O my soul!

For me, be it Christ, be it Christ hence to live: If Jordan above me shall roll,

No pang shall be mine, for in death as in life, Thou wilt whisper Thy peace to my soul.

But Lord, 'tis for Thee, for Thy coming we wait, The sky, not the grave, is our goal;

Oh, trump of the angel! Oh, voice of the Lord! Blessed hope, blessed rest of my soul.

And Lord, haste the day when my faith shall be sight, The clouds be rolled back as a scroll;

The trump shall resound, and the Lord shall descend, Even so, it is well with my soul.

To be grievously devastated and write a beautiful hymn of praise through tears and heartache is something only God can accomplish through a heart that thanks and praises Him no matter what. As we make praising Him a priority in our lives, we then have the ability to genuinely say, *"Praise the Lord, O my soul"* (Psalm 146:1) through all that happens in life.

Something else I truly marvel at, and praise God for, is God's glorious creation. The level of His genius creativity is astounding! To be in total awe of God, all you have to do is look for evidences of His powerful majesty. As I consider all the variety in life to be grateful for, I cannot even fathom God's power. Look at nature alone—the bountiful varieties of plants, trees, flowers, animals, sea creatures, fruits and vegetables (and all other food sources), and all living things that God has created and blesses us with is absolutely phenomenal.

We get to experience the joys of different seasons every year, each with it's own beauty. From the fresh newness and beauty of Spring, to the warm sunniness of Summer, to the crisp leaves and coolness of Fall, to the glistening of a winter snow, *God made our world for us to praise Him and enjoy life.*

God could have stopped there, but He didn't because God's love is extravagant! He lavishes us with not only nature, but also the gifts of family and friends. The variety of all the unique personalities of my family and friends simply humbles and astounds me, each are truly an original masterpiece of God.

God truly enriches our lives by blessing us with variety. There is variety in every detail and facet of our lives. God could have given us the exact same type of people, food, musical style, nature, and seasons, but He didn't. *He wants us to enjoy Him, life, His variety, and His creativity to the fullest.* We have done nothing to deserve God's creative genius, yet we get the privilege of experiencing His love, creativity, and creation every single day. I'm telling you, we serve a powerful, creative, genius, majestic God who is beyond worthy of our utmost praise!

Praising God through every facet of our lives and giving Him total access to our hearts is what God will use to grow a special love relationship with us. Praising Him, showing Him our gratefulness, cultivating hearts of thankfulness, and learning the lessons He has for us allows our hearts to deeply rejoice in His goodness—through every situation.

When I go through challenging situations in life, a passage of scripture that has been so meaningful to me is found in Psalm 46, *"God is our refuge and strength, an ever-present help in trouble. Therefore we will not fear, though the earth give way and the mountains fall into the heart of the sea, though its waters roar and foam and the mountains quake with their surging. There is a river whose streams make glad the city of God, the holy place where the Most High dwells. God is within her, she will not fall; God will help her at break of day. The LORD Almighty is with us; the God of Jacob is our fortress. He says, "Be still, and know that I am God; I will be exalted among the nations, I will be exalted in the earth." The LORD Almighty is with us; the God of Jacob is our fortress."* (NIV) God truly is a refuge and strength who helps us through any and every trouble. He will not abandon, leave, or quit on us as we seek His heart. He does not tire of us or belittle our grief or pain. Though everything is falling apart in our lives, we do not need to fear our circumstances if God is with us. We can be still and trust in Him, His purposes, and His love. Yes, God truly is our refuge and strength, a very present help in times of heartache and troubles.

God desires for us to rejoice in Him, *but* He also understood that we would need a blueprint for how to accomplish this task. Philippians 4:4-9 says, *"Rejoice in the Lord always. I will say it again: Rejoice! Let your gentleness be evident to all. The Lord is near. Do not be anxious about anything, but in every situation, by prayer and petition, with thanksgiving, present your requests to God. And the peace of God, which transcends all understanding, will guard your hearts and your minds in Christ Jesus. Finally, brothers and sisters, whatever is true, whatever is noble, whatever is right, whatever is pure, whatever is lovely, whatever is admirable—if anything is excellent or praiseworthy—think about such things. Whatever you have learned or received or heard from me, or seen in me—put it into practice. And the God of peace will be with you."* (NIV) This passage of scripture outlines a specific design of how to praise God through our grief. Rejoicing is so important that God instructs us to rejoice twice in a row. We are to clothe our hearts with gentleness in how we deal with others so that God receives the glory. We do not have to go through daily anxiety when going through a challenging situation—instead, we are to offer our prayers by petitioning God with our needs and the desires of our hearts. We are to continually thank Him for all of the good in our lives, His provision, and our relationship with Him. As we go to God through our struggles and read His Word, God's peace will guard our hearts and our minds. We are to guard our hearts and minds, from discouragement and anxiety, through training our hearts and minds to think about whatever is true, noble, right, pure, lovely, admirable, and anything that is excellent and praiseworthy. God wants to teach us to fill our minds and our lives with praiseworthy things through Him because He wants good things filling our hearts and our minds. We are to practice this every single day, and as we do, He will fill us with His peace and praise.

We also can develop the fruits of the Spirit into our hearts and lives as we walk through the valleys of our grief. Galatians 5:22-23, *"But the Holy Spirit produces this kind of fruit in our lives: love, joy, peace, patience, kindness, goodness, faithfulness, gentleness, and self-control."* (NLT) As we develop love, joy, peace, patience, kindness, goodness, faithfulness, humility, and self-control into our everyday lives, we begin to develop a thankful heart of praise that truly connects with the heart of God. There is no better time than during times of grief to develop the fruits of His Spirit. In developing the fruits of the Spirit, we fall more in love with God and His amazing heart and attributes. I am convinced that if we seek God's heart, and find out for ourselves who God truly is through His Word, He will reveal Himself and His character to us. As we learn to love Him more and more, we enter into the most beautiful love relationship we could ever hope for. God is so worthy of our thankfulness, gratefulness, and praise.

Make the commitment today to develop His character into your life. Ask Him to bless you with the fruits of His Spirit. Make it a top priority to allow God total access to your heart so that He can develop thankfulness, gratefulness, and praise into your everyday life. God will be with you every step of the way. It is through a genuine relationship with Him that you will find your ability to thank and praise Him once again. He will build gratefulness, thankfulness, and praise into your heart and give you a new life song of hope.

"Heavenly Father, thank you for all of the good You allow and bless me with in my life. I'm not thankful for the loss I have experienced, but I am so very thankful for Your provision, concern, and love that You bless me with daily. Lord, help me to see the good and blessings that I still have in my life in spite of my loss. Give me a heart that praises you even in the midst of my pain and grief. Develop in me a grateful heart that truly desires to delight in You. During times of discouragement, help me to keep my mind sharp and focused, and give me the grace to put on the whole armor of God that You have supplied me with. Thank You for supplying me with Your Word, I would be lost without Your guidance. Thank You for the beauty of Your creation and the incredible variety you provide in life. I praise Your creative genius! As I deepen my relationship with you through reading Your Word, reveal to my heart truths that you have specifically for me. Develop Your heart, character, and fruits in my life, and make me more like You. Continue to heal my pain and my heart so that I may praise and thank You more and more everyday. In Jesus Name I pray, Amen."

3 Oxygens

1. Do a complete inventory of everything good in your life and think of all the people who have benefitted your life. Sit down and write thank you notes to every person who has significantly loved you or who has poured blessings into your life. Thank God for all of the good in your life, what He has done throughout your life, for the times He has delivered you, and thank Him for all that He is planning to do.

2. Develop God's character into your life. Ask Him to bless you with the fruits of His Spirit—love, joy, peace, patience, kindness, goodness, faithfulness, humility, and self-control. Think on whatever is true, whatever is noble, whatever is right,

whatever is pure, whatever is lovely, whatever is admirable, and anything that is excellent or praiseworthy.

3. Find at least 5 things to be grateful for every single day. Praise God each day for something you are truly grateful for. Through prayer and song, praise Him for His goodness. Praise Him for all of His amazing creation and His creative genius. Go to a park or zoo, watch a sunrise or sunset, and soak in all God's creativity and majesty.

Bonus Oxygen

Purchase a Bible and begin a new interactive experience with God. Read His Word everyday, underline or highlight verses He shows you, and write in the margins the truths He reveals to your heart.

CHAPTER 5

~

The Oxygen of Uniqueness

It is extremely important for everyone to realize that not everyone grieves the same way. There are so many varying levels of grief, as well as grieving styles, and *they are ALL correct.* Some cry, while some do not. Some enjoy talking about and remembering their loved one, while others do not. Some are sad or angry about their loss, while some rejoice at their loved one's Home-going because their loved one is no longer suffering due to a major illness or circumstance. Some may want others to share in their grief, while others prefer experiencing their grief alone in solitude. No grieving style or how one deals with grief is wrong, because grief is as individual and unique as the person going through a loss. Grief is a personal experience, a personal journey, so never feel bad or guilty for how you grieve or for the way you feel. *The important thing is to honorably and thoroughly go through your grief in a way that is comfortable to you so that you are eventually able to live and enjoy life once again.*

You will most likely be given much advice on how you should grieve— but pain, grief, and loss are way too personal of an experience for someone to tell you how to grieve. Never allow someone else to put you into a position of trying to get you to grieve the way they think you should grieve. This is *your* unique grief experience and nobody else's. When family or friends discourage you by being critical of your grief process, consider 2 Corinthians 10:5, *"We demolish arguments and every pretension that sets itself up against the knowledge of God, and we take captive every thought to make it obedient to Christ."* (NIV) It is of upmost importance to take every thought you have throughout your grief process captive and align it with biblical truth. One of the worst feelings I had while going through grief was when well meaning family and friends told me how I should grieve. I have found that majority of family and friends truly want to offer encouragement, but for some reason, there are always a few that tend to compound grief. When family and friends offer unsolicited advice, compare and align their advice with what God says in the Bible. During discouraging times, consider what is being said, then see for yourself what God says about it through His Word. What would God think about the advice you are being offered? When thoughts come to your mind, test them and train your mind to think with the mind of Christ. What would God think about your thoughts? It is too easy to be self-critical during times of grief or life challenges. Do not allow yourself to sabotage your grief recovery progress through self-defeating thoughts or thoughtless words by others.

Most family, friends, and grief recovery resources will be encouraging and helpful, but be sure to not allow any discouragement to take root in your heart. I remember some of the grief recovery books I had read telling me how I would or should be feeling. I simply did not feel the way they said I should feel. Not only was I going through intense emotional pain, I then felt like a failure. I felt like something was wrong with me since I wasn't feeling how I was told to feel, and I felt frustrated that I couldn't even do the grief steps in the correct order. The grief steps that are outlined in many books are very helpful and effective for a great number of people, but sadly I was not one of them. One of the reasons I decided to write this book was so that I could tell what encouraged me, what gave me comfort, and to share what personally worked for me during my times of grief. I figured that if I felt frustrated in my grief recovery efforts, that there may be others who were in need of a different approach to grief recovery too. My book may be very helpful to some, or it may not be helpful at all. Different grief recovery efforts will yield different results. Everybody is unique and should feel the freedom to grieve in their own unique way.

 Grief recovery is truly about going through grief *your* way while allowing God to heal, restore, and mend your broken heart and life. No two people are going to go through, look at, or feel grief or loss in the exact same way. We were not designed by God to be a cookie cutter people—and I believe that healing cannot be cookie cutter style either. Each person has been created by God to be unique, special, and a true individual. Each person's experiences are also unique and individual as well. Merely going through some cookie cutter style of grief recovery is not going to work for every person. Have the courage to break the cookie cutter mold, then do what is best for you and your family with God's help and His love embracing you. God knows exactly what you need as a unique individual to properly heal, so ask Him to guide and direct you.

Feel free to feel what you need to in whatever manner is best for you. Please don't allow others to make you feel frustrated or guilty where you begin to think that something is wrong with you—and please be careful not to allow well meaning people to add to your grief. As long as you are pleasing God in your grief recovery efforts, you should do what works best for you.

I think each person's grief recovery is as individualized as the situation that brought on their grief, so I encourage you to do what is best for you and your family. Cry out to God and ask Him to pave the way to what is best for you and your family, your hearts, and your lives. Grieving takes time so be patient and work thoroughly through your grief.

Unlike other life events, you have no control and absolutely no choice when it comes to dealing with death and loss. With death, it is horrifically permanent. There is nothing you can do to immediately make it better. When we go through loss, majority of the time, we don't get to pick what happens, or choose the ensuing circumstances and feelings that accompany the loss. With grief, we don't get to choose when it hits us, and we don't get to choose when it ends. When loss, death, and grief happens, it is there when you wake up in the morning . . . it lingers with you throughout the day . . . and it is still there when you go to sleep at night. The remembrance of your loved one or loss shows up in the most unexpected places. It shows up uninvited, without warning in multiple situations. For example, it may show up in the car when your loved one's favorite song comes on the radio. It shows up as you pass by your loved one's favorite restaurant or you come upon a cherished photo. When you're dealing with other losses, such as a job loss, you find yourself running into old colleagues at public places. If you're dealing with the devastating loss of a marriage, or are dealing with the painful loss of adultery, it just so happens that you run into your ex and their new love interest, former family members, or the affair partner. If you have lost quality of life due to a physical situation, just the mere thought of not being able to enjoy what you previously could haunts you day and night. If your loss was sexual abuse, all it takes is someone hugging you the wrong way, a certain fragrance, or even a simple remembrance of the event that will sink you into possible tears, depression, and anxiety. Regardless of whatever situation of loss you are going through, uninvited remembrances of grief can leave you feeling powerless, depressed, and helpless.

How does one deal with the pain of loss? Does it ever go away? When will you feel better? When I have gone through times of grief, I often asked not *when*, but *if* I would ever feel "normal," much less better. It *is* possible to feel better, so please take heart and know that there is hope. Even though you cannot control your grief, you are so much more in control than you think. Nobody gets to choose what hurt or loss they go through in life—but each person *can* choose how they respond to each and every situation they face. With God's help, we can properly respond to our pain. Even the most tragic circumstances can be made into something of great value.

Another unique trait of healing through grief is thoroughly mourning a loved one's life and death. When someone you love dies, the grief you experience may be complex. You don't just grieve a person's death, you grieve every aspect of their life. I have grieved for my sister on so many different levels throughout the years. I grieved for her as my sister, as my friend, as her children's mother, and I grieved her as a gifted pianist. When my sister's daughters reached special milestones in their lives, it was bittersweet. It was so special and amazing that I got to be a part of their lives, but I mourned that their mom couldn't share in their joys and successes while growing up. Throughout the years, I grieved when my sister couldn't attend special events in my life. It broke my heart that my sister wasn't able to be there on my wedding day, especially since she and I had talked about her being in my wedding the last time I saw her alive. The last conversation we had, we talked about her being my matron of honor. It was very hard not having her, or her daughters, at my wedding to share in my joy. I also grieved my sister's talent; I was surprised by how much I missed hearing my sister play the piano. My sister was a very accomplished pianist with concert playing ability. Growing up, I would hear her playing constantly in preparation for contests and recitals. Even after she was married, she'd still play the piano when she came to visit. I missed hearing my sister play, and if I hear a song she played, it still brings her to mind. I remember the time she was able to sit down at the piano and play Frédéric Chopin's *Fantaisie Impromptu* perfectly on her first try, just by reading the sheet music. Every time I hear that song, I think of both my sisters since they both have played it. Throughout the years, I have grieved the fact that my sister was not able to be a part of her daughters' lives. She was the best mom and it pains me that they never had the opportunity to know just how truly wonderful and exceptional their mom was. Grieving takes time as there are so many details, talents, and events that need to be grieved in addition to grieving a loved one's life.

As I said before, there is not any one particular *right* way to grieve. On the opposite side of the coin, the only *wrong* way to grieve is to simply not deal with it at all, or to harm yourself or those around you during your grief process. Believe me, ignoring your loss is very tempting to superficially resolve your grief, but it will only leave you with guilt, frustration, and heartache. It is imperative that you find a way to resolve your grief to the best of your ability and allow the pain to work its purpose—if not for yourself, then for those around you.

When we go through grief, we do not have to allow our grief to control us. We can choose to be God-guided throughout our grief process. I've seen two women go through the horrific pain of losing a young adult child to sudden deaths without warning. The first woman chose to be Grief-controlled, allowing her grief to slowly destroy her life. She became emotionally void, detaching herself from her spouse, grandchildren, and stopped living life. Her grief convinced her to stay in a continual depressed state for over 30 years. Designing her own protective cocoon of denial and bitterness, she isolated herself, and lost out on over 30 years of memories which compounded her guilt, loss, and regret. She gave total control over to her grief, allowing her pain, guilt, and bitterness to control every ounce of the shell that she called life after her child died.

The second woman, as excruciating and hard as it was, chose to be God-guided throughout her grief. As she trusted God, she chose to live life in honor of her child by loving and living for her family and grandkids. She made the decision to allow God to make a new life and new memories for herself and her family. She did not simply forget her child or get over what happened—*she made a conscious decision to live life in spite of her loss.* When loss happens, you NEVER "get over" what pierced you with the ultimate utmost pain, rather you learn how to breathe again and use a new set of life-lungs that are graciously offered to you by God through His healing.

Are you concerned that you won't ever be able to move forward? Please think about the following analogy:

Imagine that you are in a building that is on fire. When you're in a situation of fire, you have several choices. You could crawl and escape out of the building to safety, you could call the fire department from another location or your cell phone, you could use a fire extinguisher, or worse case scenario, you could crawl into a closet, hide, and deny there's a fire. Grief is just like a fire. So many people, deep in their grief, choose to deny their grief recovery by simply hiding their pain, giving up all hope, and dying more and more every single day. Would it be wise, or the best choice, to lay down and die in the fire if you had a fighting chance of survival? Would it be acceptable to take on the attitude of, *"The building is on fire, but if I think it will just go away, then it will not really be happening"* . . . denying it's existence? What if there were other family members or friends in that blazing building? Grief is a lot like this analogy. Grief is a monumental fire that, if not properly dealt with, has the potential to further destroy every part of your life that the original loss was merciful enough to leave behind.

Like the fire analogy, you have decisions to make in your grieving process. Choose to deal with your grief head-on and make your grief experience your own individual process. If you feel like crying, then cry—and cry as hard and loud as you want. If you don't feel like crying, then DO NOT feel guilty about it. The tears might be there from the very first moment you hear of your loss or they may not show up until an unexpected time after the initial numbness wears off. Trust me, the grieving will happen on your own individual time table. The first moment I learned of my sister's death, I began crying. As I drove away from the hospital parking lot, I broke down heavily in excruciating pain. I cried and screamed in sheer anguish all the way home from the hospital. After that long drive home, crying was sporadic. I never knew when the tears would surface. Sometimes the tears would be there for days, then suddenly I wouldn't cry for weeks. Crying truly came about after I woke up to the reality that she was never coming back. Ignoring my grief certainly compounded it later. During the times that I didn't cry, I felt like something was wrong with me, I felt as though maybe I didn't love or miss my sister enough. Crying and grieving do not necessarily prove the depth of your love or the amount you miss someone. Sometimes, you have either outcried yourself so the tears can no longer form or crying simply isn't your grieving style. Never gauge your level of love for someone or your level of missing someone with the amount of tears you cry, for tears are a faulty indicator.

Returning back to the analogy of the fire, other family members are also dealing with this horrendous monstrous fire called grief. Be compassionate, encouraging, and available to each other. Grief is easier to handle when the burden of it is shared among trusted, caring family members and friends. Key word here is *trusted*. I caution you to be careful who you confide in when it comes to any issue of loss. The last thing you want to have to deal with is someone betraying your trust and confidence. If you have been through heavy grief, you do not need the extra burden of worrying if someone is going to share your grief experience with others.

I warn you because I have felt the sting of betrayal and it made me want to isolate myself. I have learned through grief and hardships who I can trust and who I cannot. I'm not saying to not trust anyone because there are people who truly want to encourage you and help you through your grief. I'm simply saying to be careful. Please use discernment and wisdom when sharing your heartache to avoid feeling hurt or betrayed.

Grief and loss have definitely become second nature in the lives of our family, but the valuable lessons we each have uniquely learned through grief are priceless. As my sister (who lost two fiancés) now says, *"You can't buy life lessons on grief at Walmart."* I can honestly say that I am grateful for the unique lessons I have learned along the way. I would never have chosen to go through the heartaches I have experienced, but grief is an excellent teacher on life lessons. The lessons I have learned have added a depth and compassion that I never could have achieved had I not been through loss. More importantly, I could never have developed the depth of intimacy I have with God had I never gone through grief.

Loss comes in all sorts of shapes, sizes, and situations. Some losses are temporary while some losses are so severe and permanent that it becomes impossible to get back the original breath you once breathed. You must ask God for a new breath of life if you are to effectively resolve hurt, bitterness, and painful issues in your heart and life. There have been plenty of times that God has had to be my "ventilator" and breathe for me until I could breathe once again on my own.

Regaining your ability to "breathe" and live life once again will demand that you address your grief head-on. You can no longer ignore your loss, you can no longer be a resident in fantasy land. It's time to deal with your grief and pain so that you can begin to have the ability to live life fully once again. If I had not dealt effectively with my grief, I would be a Grief-controlled basket case right now. Only when I sought God and addressed my grief head-on did I begin to make true lasting progress.

As I said earlier, your feelings are uniquely yours. When you ask God to help you through your grief, He allows you to intuitively know what you need, and what it is going to take to get you to a place of genuine healing. All the advice in this book, or any other grief recovery book, is simply what personally helped the author through their grief or loss. Some advice will be helpful, some might not be. Everybody processes grief and loss very uniquely. There is no one-size-fits-all when dealing with grief. One of the things I appreciate about going through a grief experience with God is that it becomes a unique experience. It isn't about grief recovery steps, how-to, or a timetable. I appreciate how grieving with God breaks the cookie cutter mold of grief. There is no formula for grief recovery, it is a highly individualized experience. I know that grief recovery will be one of the hardest things you will have to experience in life, but with God's help, I know you will find the strength and the courage you will need to create a better quality of life for yourself and your loved ones. I admire you and applaud your courage as you make necessary time with God to re-learn how to breathe. He truly knows what you need in your time of grief and genuinely cares about you.

If you doubt that you were uniquely made, or that God cares about you, read and consider the following two scripture passages:

Matthew 10:30, *"He pays even greater attention to you, down to the last detail—even numbering the hairs on your head!"* (MSG)

God cares about you so much that He knows every detail about you, even knowing precisely how many hairs are on top of your head! If He knows you to that great of a detailed level, you can trust Him to know in greater detail how to heal your heart and help you through your grief.

Psalm 139:13-18, *"Oh yes, you shaped me first inside, then out; you formed me in my mother's womb. I thank you, High God—you're breathtaking! Body and soul, I am marvelously made! I worship in adoration—what a creation! You know me inside and out, you know every bone in my body; You know exactly how I was made, bit by bit, how I was sculpted from nothing into something. Like an open book, you watched me grow from conception to birth; all the stages of my life were spread out before you, The days of my life all prepared before I'd even lived one day. Your thoughts—how rare, how beautiful! God, I'll never comprehend them! I couldn't even begin to count them— any more than I could count the sand of the sea. Oh, let me rise in the morning and live always with you!"* (MSG)

God not only knows how many hairs are on your head, He knows you completely inside and out. You are a unique creation made exclusively by Him. He knew exactly what your entire life story was, *start to finish,* before you even breathed one breath. He designed the entirety of your life and knew every heartache you would face throughout that design. Your heartbreaking situation did not come as a surprise to Him. In fact, He knows exactly what it will take to bring you to the point of peace and an ability to live true life once again. Your experience with grief is as unique as you. Embrace your unique grief experience and make it your own. Draw close to the One who holds the answers to your grief recovery. You can make it through this!

Matthew 11:28-30, *"Come to me, all you who labor and are heavy laden, and I will give you rest. Take My yoke upon you and learn from Me, for I am gentle and lowly in heart, and you will find rest for your souls. For My yoke is easy and My burden is light."* (NKJV)

"Heavenly Father, I praise you for making me a unique individual and for caring about each and every detail that is going on in my life. Lord, I thank You that You have already designed a personalized, unique grief recovery plan just for me. Guide me through my grief as I trust You to work in my heart and life. I ask you to fill me with Your Holy Spirit and ask You to pour Your love, encouragement, and comfort into my heart. Help me to see my grief experience through Your eyes and not my limited worldly viewpoint. If You care to know how many hairs are on my head then I realize the truth that You care about me so much more than I can humanly comprehend. Thank You for creating me to be a unique special person with true individuality. Reveal to my heart the best ways to grow through my grief experience and give me Your grace to truly find how to live my life fully once again. Thank you that I can trust You, Lord. In Jesus Name, Amen"

3 Oxygens

1. Realize that your grief process is uniquely yours. Thoroughly go through your grief, with God, in a way that is comfortable to you so that you are eventually able to live and enjoy life once again.

2. Practice taking every advice you are given, and every thought you have, throughout your grief process captive and align it with biblical truth.

3. Ask God to help you make the transition from being Grief-controlled into being uniquely God-guided throughout your grief.

Chapter 6

~

The Oxygen of
Faith & Hope

In each grief experience I have faced, faith and hope have been important factors in healing from intense grief. Faith and hope are acquired through a solid relationship with God, and trusting His purpose and plan. Faith and hope go hand in hand—God has designed each with the purpose of helping you through your grief. Hebrews 11:1 says, "*Faith is the confidence that what we hope for will actually happen; it gives us assurance about things we cannot see.*" (NLT)

Hope is realizing that no matter how you are presently feeling, there will eventually be a day that you are going to feel better. Faith is knowing that God is in control and that He has a purpose for your pain. Hope and faith together is realizing that there will be many hard roads, and you will have to go through intense pain to get to the other side, but if you allow God to perfect His purpose in and through your life, there is a bigger purpose that will eventually be revealed.

Imagine if you will that Grief is a city with many roads. As you are driving your car in the city you normally call Life, all of a sudden the road merges into the city of Grief. There is no other alternate route, you must take the detour to Grief. Some roads in the city of Life merge you into the city of Grief because another driver in a car blindsided you and forced you to merge into Grief (death of a loved one due to crime or suicide, injury, being laid off at work, abandonment, being rejected by parents or family members through no fault of your own, dealing with the addiction of a spouse or family member, sexual assault, adultery or betrayal by your spouse, etc).

Some roads that merge you into the city of Grief are caused by direct disobedience or foolishness due to your own decisions (losing a marriage due to mistreatment of your spouse or infidelity, disability or illness from lack of caring for personal health, accident or disability due to foolish decisions, poor financial or business decisions, marital or family disharmony due to your pride or unwise personal decisions, etc).

Other roads merge you into the city of Grief due to acts of nature or the devil (death of a loved one, natural disasters, illness, war, terrorist attacks, etc). All of these avenues of Grief (whether allowed by God, or caused by the devil, another person, or your own decisions) are very painful. No matter the cause, every situation has one common denominator—every situation of grief needs God's healing and His divine intervention if there is to be any true long-lasting relief from the pain.

You will need to trust God to guide you in your travels in the city of Grief. It is He who has the power to help you find the road that takes you back to the city of Life. Once in the city of Grief, if you turn onto the unending roads of bitterness or depression, you will be stuck in Grief and remain there. If you simply quit, you will become a permanent resident of Grief. You will need to do whatever is needed to get you back to the city of Life. You will never forget the detour and journey you had to go through while in Grief, but you *can* make it back to Life. God is the ultimate GPS while traveling in the city of Grief. When you place your faith and hope in Him, He is faithful to guide and direct you through the streets of Grief until you arrive back to Life. Once in Life again, God is faithful to fulfill His purpose for your life.

Consider this: when you travel somewhere, you understand how you arrived at a destination, the roads that were beneficial, and how to best navigate through a destination. Grief is the exact same. When you have made the transition of traveling from Grief back to Life, you have the ability to help guide others to do the same. You have the ability to offer hope and direction when others face difficulties.

I once was forced to merge into the city of Grief. I went through a horribly painful loss that made absolutely no sense whatsoever. There was nothing good about this loss and it rendered me extremely heartbroken for awhile. I could see no future good coming from the loss—all I could see was my intense pain. The pain was so terrible that I didn't think I would ever recover from my pain . . . I felt as though I had lost my hope. While trying to navigate through my grief, I made a decision to choose faith over feelings. I submitted to God and asked Him to reveal His purpose and plan for what had happened. I'm not going to sit here and say that as soon as I submitted to God that a great light appeared from the sky and soon everything was rainbows and cotton candy—because that isn't how God or life works. I will tell you that as soon as I submitted to God, I was able to enter into His suffering. I then was able to relate with Him at a very deep emotional and spiritual level. I wouldn't have had the opportunity to experience a deeper relationship with Him without going through this particular loss. During this loss, God truly restored my hope as I ran to Him in my heartache. It was through this particular grief journey that I was able to see grief and loss in a whole new light. I can't even begin to describe the many lessons about faith, true forgiveness, hope, genuine love, and suffering that I learned through this specific grief experience. I can't explain how God worked through my heart and spirit to get me to the place of grace He brought me to, or how He restored my hope and joy—all of the credit goes to Him. In my human nature, I would have chosen depression and bitterness. The moment I cried out to God in my pain, He and I began a grief journey together that was custom designed by Him to help me to travel where He needed me to be. As I trusted and submitted to God during this difficult time, He was faithful to give me an extra measure of His grace to have the ability to forgive and heal. I learned so much through this trial about God's love, character, and fruits of His Spirit by allowing Him full access to change my heart through developing His love, character, and fruits in my life. I learned how to truly live life to the fullest in spite of my grief and how to genuinely allow God to develop His plan and purpose for my life. Ultimately, I found how to love God more and received a new depth of God's love as He carried me through the storms of this trial. *That is what grief is truly about—diving into a deeper love relationship with God, allowing Him to work in and through our lives for His greater purposes as He teaches us to live a fuller life.* I never thought I would ever fully heal from that particular grief experience, but what *we* think is impossible is very possible with *God*. Matthew 19:26 says, *"But Jesus looked at them and said, With men this is impossible, but all things are possible with God."* (AMP) Having a deeper relationship with God, having our hearts continually transformed, and recovering from our grief is possible because of Him.

Grief molds us into the image of Christ as we allow Him to write and shape our grief story and grief recovery. The most important thing about life is your relationship with God—and He will allow whatever is necessary for you to experience faith, hope, love, and His heart in the deepest ways possible. God sometimes allows really wonderful things to happen to draw us close to His heart, while other times He allows painful circumstances so that we will understand faith, hope, and His heart at a deeper level. He is a God of love, compassion, mercy, strength, and justice. The more grief you go through, as well as the wonderful blessings God brings into your life, the richer the opportunities you will have to truly know His heart and mind. By running to Him during times of joy, as well as in times of sorrow, pain, and frustration, a solid relationship and foundation is built to equip us with the faith and hope we will need throughout life. God has shown me time and time again that genuine faith, hope, and joy are direct blessings of grief and loss.

Grief is a one way ticket to knowing God fuller and that is exactly why we are here on earth—to know and love God to the fullest and best of our abilities. The rewards, depth, blessings, wisdom, and treasures you receive while walking with God through your grief are priceless. Grief is a customized gift from God and the treasures you can glean from your journey is something that only God Himself can reveal to your heart. It requires faith to be able to see this truth. I am *not* saying that the situation of loss that brought on your grief is a gift. Loss hurts horrifically deep and there isn't a loss in life that can be called a gift. However, the *benefits* you receive through grief *are* a gift because you're growing closer to the heart of God. Some of the benefits I have received during my times of grief are a closer relationship with God and my family. I now realize that life is short and the days are evil so I understand that people or opportunities could die at any time without warning. My grief has taught me to celebrate the good things in life everyday. Another gift through grief's lessons has been a deepening of my faith and a renewed hope. Grief has taught me that I have an internal strength that I wasn't aware I had and to be wise in my decisions. Grief has taught me a deep compassion and empathy for family and friends that I never would have developed had grief never been a part of my life. All of these are "gifts" that I obtained through my grief.

All things are possible through God and He is more than able to restore and heal your broken heart, faith, hope, joy, and life. When you are in the midst of grieving, this is what you need to hear. Pause right now and ask God to give you the gifts of faith, hope, joy, and love through your grief process. Ask Him to reveal His heart, His amazing comfort, and His purposes for you. Your mind and feelings will tell you that this is not what you need, but your heart and faith will reveal that this is exactly what you need to be able to effectively overcome your grief. If you are to have a brand new perspective on life, you will need God's gifts of faith, hope, joy, and love. My definition of overcoming grief is *to once again live a productive life, where life can once again have purpose, meaning, joy, and pleasure.* I am not saying that you will overcome your grief in the sense that you will forget about your loss or loved one. Grief never goes away completely, *but* it does change over time. It becomes more bearable over time—and eventually, it will not be continually present and painful. Whether your loss is a death, a divorce, an assault, the loss of a dream, family or marital conflict, or any other source of grief, painful memories will exist. I will never lose the painful memories of losing someone I greatly loved or lose the memories of other painful losses I have experienced. However, I am able to live life to the fullest in spite of loss due to making the decision to place my faith and hope in God. I choose by faith to trust His purpose for every situation I have been through. I do not like what He has allowed me to go through—*but by faith*—I can be grateful for each grief experience He has entrusted to me because of the lessons I have learned and the testimony He has developed in my heart. We are able to overcome our grief as we turn our eyes and focus away from our grief and onto God.

Faith is saying to God, "Your will, not mine," for we were created to do His good works and not our own. There has been such an amazing freedom in giving God my life and my heart, trusting Him with His promise of Romans 8:28, *"And we know that all things work together for good to those who love God and are called according to His purpose."*

(NKJV) I no longer have to carry the burden of working my life out, that is God's responsibility. The responsibilities I now have are loving God and obeying His word—the rest is up to Him. When I mention the word faith, I am not advocating a blind faith that says whatever happens, you should just simply trust God and feel joyful at all times. With grief, feelings are unpredictable and joy is something that is produced by God and perfected by God over time. You are probably not going to immediately feel joyful while going through loss, especially if this is your first experience with grief. You may still have the ability to feel times of joy, but that probably is not going to be the norm. Grief is incredibly hard, it bites like a cold day in winter. There are going to be times of great struggling and sadness, but allow God full access to your heart to develop your faith, hope, and joy.

Going through times of struggle, wrestling with what has happened, losing a loved one, feeling hopeless, or going through times of depression does not mean that you are ungodly or that you lack faith. It means you are human. God understands that you are struggling and He doesn't hold it against you. He loves you deeply and desires the best for you. He wants to help you, comfort you, and guide you through your grief. He deeply desires to reveal His love and His nature to you during times of bereavement.

God truly provides the gifts of hope, faith, and encouragement throughout His Word. In the Bible, David was beautifully transparent while writing about his intense grief. David allowed God to develop his faith and hope as he wrote about his struggles and heartaches in the Psalms. God bestowed on David the ultimate compliment: *God called David a man after His own heart.* I appreciate reading the Psalms during times of loss because the Psalms are filled with emotion, as well as an understanding of where I am in my grief process. The Psalms offer hope and the truth of God's faithfulness. It is so important for you to build a strong foundation on God and His promises, and Psalms is an excellent starting point while going through grief. Proverbs is also an excellent book to read while going through grief. Filled with wisdom, Proverbs is great for guidance throughout every facet of life. During your time of grief, others around you may attempt to compromise your faith, frustrate you, or mislead you into thinking something that is not based on truth. I strongly advise that you invest quality time in God's

Word so that you will know precisely what you think and believe based on His truth and not the mere opinions of others.

I had well meaning friends question my faith, saying I wasn't trusting in God because I wasn't rejoicing that my sister was in Heaven. I have also had others tell me that I was wrong to question God in my anguish. One even said I was selfish to want my sister to be here instead of with God. You may find that people offer ridiculous amounts of opinion, advice, and clichés during times of loss. People have done this for years, just read the book of Job. For some reason when you go through a heartbreaking situation, people feel the freedom to share and express uninvited opinions. It is in those moments that you may need to excuse yourself and get alone with God for some fresh encouragement. I remember being so hurt and frustrated when I was told to *"get over"* my sister just a few months after she had died. I wasn't wrong to not be over her. It took me 20 years to know her and love her, I wasn't going to be over her in a few months, a few years, or ever. It is not wrong to wish that your loved one was still here, that is a very natural response to losing someone you love. You are going to miss them very much and it is not a sin to miss somebody. I am happy that my loved ones are enjoying being with God but I'm not going to lie—if I could have the benefits I have learned through grief and magically have my loved ones come back to earth, I would want them to be enjoying life with me like once before. I *will* say that those that questioned my faith had never been through the loss of an immediate family member and maybe that is why they were uncomfortable with my grief. When others could not understand the depths of my grief, I found comfort in the fact that God did. God understands the fact that you are hurting. He also understands that you are desperate for any hope or faith you can muster while going through your grief. He wants to be your ultimate source for filling your heart with faith and hope.

God desires for you to thoroughly work through your grief, and I believe an important part of that is to pour your heart out to Him, telling Him how you truly feel, or telling Him that you don't understand. Ask Him questions, He is the only One with answers. He understands your pain. Respectfully lay your questions at His feet, ask Him to help you to work through your grief, and plead with Him to be glorified through you. *Your pain at the present moment has a bigger purpose than you can even begin to imagine.* I do not know what grief journey you are on or the circumstances that you are going through. There are so many circumstances as to why people are going through grief. I *do* know that God desires to bless you with the faith and hope you need so that you are eventually able to have a <u>full life</u> and <u>praise Him</u>. Psalm 71:14, *"As for me, I will always have hope; I will praise you more and more."* (NIV) Having your faith and hope restored so that you are able to genuinely praise God will become a reality for you as you open yourself up to trusting God through faith.

Some of the most inspiring life changing stories of hope I have ever heard have been from those who have gone through intense grief. Their testimony of how they put their faith and hope in God for the outcome of their grief is truly inspirational—and an excellent example of a heart that trusts God. As I mentioned earlier, one particular amazing role model of placing hope and faith in God is Horatio Spafford, who is best known for writing the hymn It Is Well With My Soul. My heart broke whenever I heard about the deep grief he had experienced. In the midst of his grief, Horatio wrote this hymn after losing all of his children and majority of his earthly wealth. Mr. Spafford's ability to see God's hand, love, and goodness in spite of intense grief is a strong testament of what God's healing hand can accomplish. That is an important goal for every person who is going through grief—to see God's hand, love, and goodness during times of grief, to love Him while submitting to Him, and trusting His purpose and plan. If you are to truly get through your grief, you have got to believe with all of your heart that God does indeed have a loving purpose and plan for your life. Grief recovery is extremely hard work, filled with pain and suffering, but it is your faith and hope in God's love that will carry you through. Never doubt God's concern for you—His empathy for you is great and He genuinely desires to build your faith and hope.

Faith, hope, love, and perseverance are tools that God uses to mold His character into our lives, especially during times of grief. We have such a high need of feeling as though everything in our life is good, as well as comfortable, and we panic the very moment things are turned upside down. We can sense with our God-given intuition and feelings that something isn't right and we begin to try to make everything alright as quickly as we can. We become intensely uncomfortable with grief because it goes against our entire nature. We simply cannot control it. It is always painful when God allows your heart to be stretched out of your comfort zone as He develops faith, hope, and His character in your life—*but what if the pain He allows in your life increases the flexibility of ways He is then able to use you?* What if the pain you are experiencing is for a greater purpose than you can presently comprehend?

Reflecting on each trial I have experienced, I can now clearly see that grief is intertwined with faith. God has a purpose for each and every pain we go through, but it is up to us to seek Him—and not turn to other things during our times of heartache. Don't be surprised if you are tempted to turn to things other than God to bring relief during your grief process. Some people have multiplied their grief by not starting off seeking God for His help and comfort. I know of too many people that have given in to the temptations of addictions, prescription pills, alcohol, drugs, or other substances to feel temporarily better. Some may be tempted to begin an addiction of excessive busyness or shopping, denial, overeating, or another addiction so that they will not have to feel their grief and heartache so strongly. *Addictions and substances have a false appearance of having the ability to heal your pain and make you feel better—but when all is said and done, you will have multiplied your grief and will have brought even more loss into your life.* Somebody close to my heart chose to indulge in prescription medicines in response to her grief. She was very angry at God for allowing her adult child to die. She wasn't wrong to be angry about her child's death because I think anyone who has lost a child has been angry and tremendously devastated by their child's passing. Losing a child is a devastating, horrific experience. This woman was not wrong for her pain but she was foolish for becoming hooked on prescription drugs. The prescription drugs hindered her from being able to fully function in life and added much pain to her husband and family. At the end of her life, she realized that she not only had lost her son, she lost precious time with her husband, remaining family, and grandchildren due to how she responded to her grief. Right before she passed away, she shared with me that she regretted the times she hadn't been there for her husband and grandchildren. She shared with me that she had been so depressed and angry with God over her child's death. She said something else I'll never forget—she said she wished she would have known how to have more faith in God during trials. She sincerely regretted a lifetime of quarreling with God, taking her pain out on her husband, and wasting the remainder of her life.

The oxygens of faith and hope are absolutely vital to your long term healing process. The challenge is that most do not want to choose faith and hope during times of grief. It is difficult to choose faith and hope when so many conflicting feelings are bombarding you during situations of grief and loss. Faith and hope simply do not feel "right" during heartache, they go against our human nature. So many feelings come out at a time of grieving. Many feelings are exactly what you would expect to feel, some are foreign feelings that will surprise you. When my sister passed away, I was surprised by my feelings of discouragement and anger. I have never been a discouraged or angry person by nature, but the finality and unfairness of her death really brought feelings of intense anger to the surface. I was also surprised how discouraged I was by the thoughtless advice I received from others. I quickly grew tired of hearing clichés—it seemed that everyone I knew suddenly became expert philosophers. What further upset me was hearing other people say ridiculously insensitive statements to my mom and sister such as, *"At least you have other children,"* or *"It's not like you won't find another fiancé, you're young."* With each insensitive comment, I became ticked . . . it hurt to see my mom and sister having their grief mocked and compounded. Yes, my mom had other children, but there was only *one* of my sister. *She wasn't replaceable.* Yes, my other sister was young enough to find love again, but that didn't take away the fact that she dearly loved the fiancé she was engaged to . . . she had wanted to spend the rest of her life *with him*. Going through grief will definitely develop graciousness, mercy, and manners in your life. Someone told me after my sister died that, *"Loss will either make you or break you."* Another told me that, *"God needed an extra special friend, that's why He took your sister."* Then another shared, *"God must have needed another angel."* While others insisted—this seemed to be everybody's favorite cliché —*"You're sister is in a better place."* With each offering of a cliché or unsolicited advice, I could hardly believe how unthoughtful people were . . . until I remembered that I had spoken clichés in the past before my sister died. It is bad judgment to speak a cliché but we all have probably done so in a feeble attempt to make a loved one feel better. I began to see that people were not meaning to discourage or upset me. No, they were only human and had no idea what to say to me in my grief.

I began to seek to understand what people were trying to communicate through their advice and I came to some conclusions: loss will break you to pieces at first, but it is totally what you do with the aftermath that will help you to make it . . . it didn't have to be one or the other. God didn't need a special friend or an extra angel, that's not why He called my sister Home . . . it was simply her time to die. Yes, my sister was lucky to be in a better place, but if she was given a choice before dying, she would have wanted more time with her daughters. Grief is an individualized process that definitely has the potential to build hope and faith if you respond to it correctly. It is a process because *grief is a work in progress.* It will be a great teacher that you will *never* forget. One of the purposes for grief is to teach you life lessons, so learn and let it challenge and change you for the better.

What will help you to experience hope and faith for your situation? Many things can help you: ask God to grant you clarity and to empower you . . . go on a walk and look at nature while meditating on God and the life He has given you . . . read your Bible . . . pray . . . seek to know and understand God's heart better . . . memorize and meditate on scripture . . . ask God to reveal His plans for you (if you are still alive, God still has a purpose for your life, He has a plan for your existence) . . . ask God to give you a new love for life . . . think of new activities you can learn and try . . . participate in former hobbies and activities that once brought you joy . . . read biographies about Christians who have triumphed over loss and found a deeper relationship with God through their trials . . . watch inspirational movies that tell of how people regained their faith and hope. There are so many ways to experience hope and faith while going through grief.

If you lost someone close to you, go to a park and reflect on your happy times together. You may want to gather pictures, cards, and other mementos to make a memory book. You may want to plant a tree in memory and honor of a loved one. If you were assaulted, take a self defense class and begin lifting weights to strengthen yourself and get the frustration out. If you lost big in business, then clear your mind and think of a way to get back to vibrancy and success. If your loss was your marriage or relational in nature, then pray, asking God for His help and power. Next, try to repair what was broken. If after you have tried your hardest to fix the problem and issues, and nothing has improved, then you will have to leave it in God's hands and trust Him as you obey His Word.

After a time of mourning your loss, find and take classes that interest you, participate in fun activities with family and friends, join a civics group, get involved in your community, volunteer, or rekindle a formerly loved hobby. Something that has helped me tremendously in times of grief is expressing creativity—keeping a journal, expressing my ideas through writing lyrics, reading and writing poetry, listening to music, going to concerts, looking at art, cooking, baking, and scrapbooking—these have all helped me through my grief. God gives us His gift of creativity and blesses us with activities to help us through our grief. Ask God to guide and direct you to activities that will bring you hope and healing. We truly can experience hope and His love through creativity and activities. With any loss, please know that God wants to be the greatest source of love, encouragement, and provision in your life. Learn to ultimately find contentment in your relationship with God, being grateful for His guidance in your life. 1 Timothy 6:6 says, *"But godliness with contentment is great gain. For we brought nothing into the world, and we can take nothing out of it."* (NIV)

If you are struggling right now, that's okay. Everybody struggles when being faced with grief or loss. It shakes our existence to the core and throws us onto an unfamiliar painful path. Do whatever you can to develop faith and hope in your life, even if it's just little steps every day. You've got to keep your faith and hope alive!

When my dad passed away, my mom thought her life was over. She was madly in love with my dad and after he passed away, she was extremely distraught. Five years after my dad passed away, my mom met her current husband at church. They have been happily married now for over 30 years. She never thought finding love again was a possibility while going through her intense grief, but she is a great example of someone fighting for her breath and getting her oxygen back. She put her faith and hope in God after losing my dad. She poured herself and her love into God, and as a result, He blessed her. She began reading her Bible everyday, falling in love with God more and more, treasuring the scripture He supplied her with daily.

One of my favorite verses about hope is Jeremiah 29:11-13. As you read it, allow it to take root deep within your heart. God desires for you to have faith, hope, prosperity, and a future. *"For I know the plans I have for you," declares the LORD, "plans to prosper you and not to harm you, plans to give you hope and a future. Then you will call upon me and come and pray to me, and I will listen to you. You will seek me and find me when you seek me with all your heart"* (NIV)

It is absolutely vital for you to find something that will bring you hope or you'll die more and more every single day. I appeal to you to find hope and a reason for living, even more so if you have children. When my dad died, my mother was only in her twenties with four small children to take care of. My mom was desperate to feel better from the pain—she realized that she had to learn how to find hope. She found her hope in God, as well as her children, and it is amazing what kind of a person she is today. She is my greatest role model for grief recovery. She's a strong, independent, beautiful, wonderful person. It truly amazes me that after going through the deaths of her husband, both of her parents, her daughter, her brother, among other serious losses, that she made it out of the city of Grief. She loves the Lord with all her heart and she is a walking testimony to her family and friends of God's healing. She is who she is today because *she refused to allow her heart or spirit to die along with each loved one that died.* She pushed forward to find hope and had a strong faith in God. It certainly wasn't easy, but God developed a strong testimony in her life.

You may be struggling to find hope or faith due to whatever loss you faced. It is very easy to feel isolated and depressed . . . to just want to give up and quit. When you have given it your all and things get worse, your world crumbling all around you, where do you find hope? You may be thinking, *"I've already tried everything I can"* or *"I feel as if I've died . . . I don't even have the energy to find my way out of bed, much less find hope."* I'm not going to tell you that I know how you feel, because I don't. I will say that in my own experiences with grief I have found that it is vital to give God total access to my heart, allowing Him to mold me for His purpose by going through the hard emotions . . . whether I feel like it or not. You have to keep on keeping on if you are to restore your hope and faith. I know that's hard, especially for those who have gone through intense grief or trauma.

My living sister has been through having her hope and faith shattered twice after going through the grief experiences of two separate fiancés dying, each within a month after they became engaged. Her first fiancé had been in the hospital for a year after a horrible car accident. He died after fighting for his life during that heartbreaking year. My sister was absolutely exhausted from going up to the hospital, working, going to college, and participating in scholarship programs. After a year of suffering, her fiancé died, and this was crushingly hard on her. While grieving the death of her fiancé, our other sister suddenly died. Needless to say, she didn't have too much hope for feeling better. My sister realized that she had to find hope, anything to get her through her grief. Several years after these deaths, after she had healed from the loss of our sister and her first fiancé dying, she began dating a longtime friend. After six years of dating, she became engaged only to have her second fiancé die on Easter unexpectedly. To see my sister twice have to go through the heartbreaking loss of someone she loved deeply was very hard. The worst thing about watching someone go through grief is that there is nothing you can say or do to make things better for them. There is no way to make them feel better other than offering them encouragement, just *being there*, and offering hope. Talking to my sister, I asked her how she was able to get through two fiancés dying. She shared with me a verse that she says got her through the pain and hard times. The verse was Psalm 71:14, *"As for me, I will always have hope; I will praise you more and more."* (NIV) She made it a priority to have hope in her life and she never stopped trusting in God.

My brother, who is a senior pastor, once shared with me that my greatest grief experience could end up being what God could most use in my life to encourage others. I found so much hope when he shared that with me. That is exactly how you can find hope: when you understand that God has a plan and purpose for what has broken your heart. After feeling like absolutely dying through some of the losses in my life, what my brother told me made me realize that there was hope at the end of the dark dreary tunnel of grief. I have found such amazing hope and healing in the times that I have helped, encouraged, and ministered to others. Do not allow your grief to be in vain! Remember that God has a purpose for your life as well as your pain—you are now equipped to help others who have gone through the same grief and heartache— what an amazing life purpose! If you help others through their grief, you are not only helping *them*, you are also helping *every person they encounter . . . including future generations.* What a high calling! When someone goes through grief, but is never comforted, they are inclined to resort to depression and bitterness. This affects everyone in their life, especially their family. When people, who have gone through similar heartaches, offer encouragement and comfort, lives are changed for the better . . . *maybe even for eternity.*

2 Corinthians 1:3-4 says *"Praise be to the God and Father of our Lord Jesus Christ, the Father of compassion and the God of all comfort, who comforts us in all our troubles, so that we can comfort those in any trouble with the comfort we ourselves receive from God."* (NIV) There is hope to be found in that verse. Allow God to comfort you, develop your life purpose, and restore your faith and hope.

I am always amazed at the great detail God is willing to go through to orchestrate an offering of hope to us in life. A few years after my sister's death, my family and I went to a conference in Tennessee. We met a woman there who had been diagnosed with the same illness that my sister died from. The odds of this chance meeting happening were slim to none due to the fact that the disease my sister died of is extremely rare, and it rarely affects women as it is an illness that primarily targets men. As we began talking with this woman, she was telling us that once you have this disease, it begins to rot all your organs. The pain and suffering that this lady had endured was horrible. It was so interesting that God allowed this woman to make it through her illness, allowing her to be able to talk to us about her pain, to further educate us first hand about this disease. No doctors were able to give us very much information at the time of my sister's death, yet God orchestrated putting this lady in our path to talk to us about what she had been through. I was given faith and hope through meeting this woman because for the first time, I had the ability to be grateful that my sister did not have to go through an endless lifetime of suffering. I could see God's mercy and it strengthened my faith in Him that He knows best.

God allows us to be a source of hope to others. Since my mother had gone through the death of my dad at a young age, she was a very valuable source of comfort and encouragement to my sister when my sister lost both of her fiancés. My mom could honestly say to my sister, *"I am so sorry . . . I understand the pain you're going through . . . how can I help?"*

When you go through a heartbreaking experience, you have an incredible gift. You have the experience and the ability to empathize with another human being—and the ability to relate to how they feel due to having been through similar pain and heartache. When I have gone through pain and I'm needing hope, it has always helped to talk to someone who I know has been through a same or similar circumstance. When my sister passed away I really needed to talk about my loss. Well meaning individuals, who couldn't relate to my grief, would always say, *"Well, you know she's in a better place."* That was the worst thing to hear since I didn't want her in a "better place"—I wanted her to be here with her daughters, our family, and me. I noticed that when I talked to others who had been through the death of a loved one, the conversation was refreshingly void of clichés. They also didn't look away or treat me strangely. Try not to be offended when others look away awkwardly, perhaps uncomfortably, and try not to be offended if people avoid you. They have no idea how to help or respond. After all, what can someone say to a friend who loses a loved one? They know they can't make a loved one magically reappear. If you become frustrated in a person's inability to encourage or comfort you, focus on your gratefulness for the ones who understand how to offer empathy, hope, and encouragement. It is wonderful having someone understand what you're going through because they can truly offer you hope. Once you find hope, *you* are going to be an absolute gift to someone else in the midst of their pain.

After I went through one particular loss, nothing could prepare me for the ongoing feelings that I went through. I am so thankful for the people in my life who have gone through the same fears, heartache, anxiety, and loss that I experienced. They have been an invaluable resource of encouragement and wisdom to help me through my pain. God used them (and their loss) to help restore my hope and faith.

Loss cannot be avoided because life seems to have a theme of throwing one curveball of loss after another. It is up to you to learn how to grow through the lessons you learn as a result of each loss. We *cannot* control loss—but we *can* control our level of faith and hope. You may not have any control over what goes on around you, but you *do* have total control over what goes on inside you! Loss and grief seek to suck every ounce of life and breath left in you, but you don't have to succumb or give up your hope. After loss and life knock the breath out of you, you can learn to get your breath back and relearn to breathe. It is not going to *just happen,* for grief doesn't get better by wishful thinking. If you are going to relearn how to breathe life back into existence . . . and get your breath back . . . you are going to have to take steps towards hope and faith to make it a reality.

Without faith and hope, it becomes too easy to adopt a victim mentality, a sulky spirit, or a lifelong pity-party. You do not want to allow a victim mentality, sulking, or a lifelong pity-party to take root in your heart. You are stronger than you realize, and *God wants more for you than that!* God is the one who grants hope and faith. It is in Him that we find the ability to carry on, to be strengthened with faith and hope, and finally have the ability to truly live life once again.

Isaiah 40:28-31, *"Do you not know? Have you not heard? The Lord is the everlasting God, the Creator of the ends of the earth. He will not grow tired or weary, and his understanding no one can fathom. He gives strength to the weary and increases the power of the weak. Even youths grow tired and weary, and young men stumble and fall; but those who hope in the Lord will renew their strength. They will soar on wings like eagles; they will run and not grow weary, they will walk and not be faint."* (NIV)

"Lord, thank you for your great gifts of hope and faith. There are times I feel so weak and discouraged. During times of weakness or discouragement, I ask You to fill me with hope and a deep faith in You. Help me to cling to the truths of Jeremiah 29:11. You desire to give me hope and a future. Please bless me with the gift of family and friends who will encourage me to have hope and faith during my times of grief. Grant me the grace to be gracious to those that are thoughtless or insensitive. Bless them for trying to comfort me. Give me an internal strength that helps me to grow stronger every single day. Renew my strength daily through time with You. When I want to lay down and quit, or throw a pity-party, do not allow that. During those times, strengthen my heart with Your hope. Restore faith and hope in my life so that I may eventually be a gift to others in their times of grief. Thank You for all You are doing in me and through me. In Jesus Name, Amen."

---

3 Oxygens

1. There are 31 chapters in the Book of Proverbs, 150 Psalms, and 30-31 days in a month. Read one chapter of Proverbs and five Psalms each day throughout the month and meditate on what God shares with your heart through reading His Word. Reading Psalms is so comforting while going through grief and the wisdom found in Proverbs is very beneficial in responding to loss and life challenges.

2. Express creativity while going through your grief—keep a journal, write, read poetry, listen to music, go to concerts, look at art, paint, scrapbook, cook, bake, or anything else you can think of to express creativity.

3. Watch inspirational movies and read Christian biographies of those who have triumphed over grief and loss. Allow their stories of faith and hope to encourage your heart.

CHAPTER 7

~

The Oxygen of Relationships & Community

Romans 12:15, *"Rejoice with those who rejoice; mourn with those who mourn."* (NIV)

Through my experiences with grief, I have found that relationships were so helpful in healing my heart during times of grief or loss. I have no idea where I would be without my family, friends, or church family—all are a part of the precious community God has blessed me with. Each have played an important role in encouraging me and helping me to truly enjoy life once again.

In His great compassion and wisdom, God knew people would need each other. He created family and community for times of life and loss: family, church, friendships, neighbors, as well as grief recovery counselors, programs, and organizations. Family, church, friends, neighbors, professionals, and organizations are all gifts from God, put in place to offer love, encouragement, comfort, hospitality, and help to support us in our daily lives—especially in times of grief, loss, or life challenges. God also places *you* in the lives of others so that you can love, encourage, and comfort others in life and in their times of grief.

God calls and places every person to a specific community and family—and He desires for you to use your relational skills and life experiences to engage with others. Not everyone has a supportive family to help them through their grief, so extended family, friends, and communities are a tremendous help when your family isn't available to offer encouragement and support. God designed families, communities, and relationships . . . so go to your family, extended family, church family, close friends, a grief support group, professional, pastor, counselor, or grief organization to help you through your grief. It is so very helpful to have an extension of people who know and understand what you are going through, who can offer you compassion, encouragement, help, and support. It's a nice bonus if they have been through a similar life experience or knew your loved one too. I truly appreciate having the ability to talk about my loved ones with those that also knew them. When I talk about my sister, dad, or others, it brings their memory back for a moment in time. It makes me feel better knowing that their existence meant a lot to someone else. Since my time was short-lived with my dad, I have really enjoyed hearing stories about his life from family and friends.

Another great support system is a church family. I have found that my church family has helped me through times of grief by praying for our family and offering gestures of love such as encouraging notes, recommended scriptures, or preparing meals for us after a loved one's death. I have found that someone simply being there has been very helpful too.

If you find that you do not have a community of support, pray about finding or even creating one. My sister and I, as a result of our grief, founded a grief recovery ministry, and we also host a monthly dining support group. We invite family and friends that are going through grief to have dinner with us for an evening of relaxation, food, and fun. Something I have found true about grief is that it is a universal language. If someone has been through loss, they universally understand how challenging grief truly is. At our dinners, there is an instant bond formed out of compassion and empathy. The purpose of our dinner is to offer an evening of encouragement and inspiration. Learning how to enjoy life once again is a top priority. Sometimes there are tears, *but* there is a freedom to cry if needed because everyone there understands that grief has a way of showing up at unexpected times. Everyone that attends is presently going through, or has been through, grief so we're all able to be ourselves and enjoy this monthly event. The important thing is that we're all like-minded and we're having fun. My sister and I enjoy creating an encouraging event where others can find a few hours of relief from the challenges of grief. The opportunity of sharing dinner with kindred hearts, while having an opportunity to offer encouragement, and sharing our Hope is priceless. It is truly great to have friends who understand what you are going through who you can have fun with.

Community is truly a gift from God on a national level as well. If you recall or remember national and world tragedies, such as 9/11, the Oklahoma City Bombing, military happenings, tornadoes, hurricanes, tsunamis, or other acts, you will find that God's plan for community springs into action, as people offer encouragement, help, and unity after heartbreaking situations of loss take place. When horrendous events take place, you see communities rallying together to help each other out. Churches, organizations, and people look for ways they can help their neighbors, the people in their communities, and even those in need in a far away location. Celebrities also get involved and perform benefit concerts where community comes together for a great cause. It is simply amazing to see the generosity, compassion, and love in people who find ways to help out where needed: praying, gathering supplies, rolling up their sleeves to help, offering their talents, or donating funds to help. It is phenomenal to see so many people compassionately reaching out to help others affected by loss at a city, state, national, or even world level. God's ultimate goal is for people to love Him, and to love and serve others through His love.

When going through loss, God develops an amazing testimony in your heart so that you can use your loss experiences, spiritual gifts, and talents to expand your ministry through serving and ministering to others. It is *not* God's plan for you to become stuck in your grief or heartache. It *is* His plan to beautifully equip you to help and minister to others. Find out His plans for your life and fulfill them. Use your grief experience, spiritual gifts, and talents to encourage and minister to others. I know it can be hard, but look outside of your pain to see how you can be a blessing and encouragement to family and friends in need. God truly can use your grief, spiritual gifts, life, personality, and talents for a greater purpose than you can imagine.

How can you best minister to your family while going through grief? If you are going through loss as a family or a couple, I encourage you to lean on each other, and be there for one another. Grief changes people so be patient and compassionate as you grieve with your spouse, children, or loved ones. Their loss may have left them guilty to feel alive, or guilty for feeling any kind of enjoyment. They need your love, support, and compassion more than ever. You may feel tempted to become impatient with your loved one's grief, or frustrated with how they are processing their loss. Don't turn away from your loved one, turn towards them in love. Don't waste time playing the blame game or isolating from each other. No amount of blame has the ability to erase your pain or change your loss. Support and encourage each other, showering each other with empathy, understanding, and love. Have faith that God will carry you and your family through every difficulty of grief. You may be *uncertain of the grief experience* you are facing, but you can be *certain of God's faithfulness* to carry you through. If you are married, take extra time and effort to care for your marriage and spouse. Divorce is prevalent after the death of a child, so it is imperative that you care for your marriage, and offer support to your spouse during their time of grief. Men and women grieve differently, so right from the start, allow each other the freedom to grieve differently—as well as the freedom to feel what each other needs to feel. Support each other and be there for one another. Honor each other's grief process and feelings. Never allow yourselves to drift apart, no matter what. If you are able, schedule one night a week to talk to your spouse and spend time with them. Go out to eat, go to a park, or stay home to talk—do not allow your marriage or family to fall apart. You may want to buy a notebook and write down topics you'd like to talk about, then talk about the topics together with your spouse every week. Also, in the notebook, write down important information, as well as your schedules. In times of grief, communication sometimes slips. A notebook helps to keep you and your spouse on the same page. Communicate, be compassionate and loving towards each other, schedule a weekly date night, set boundaries, and safeguard your marriage during grief.

If you have lost a child and have other children, be sure to have your remaining children realize how much you love them, that you are there for them, and that your sadness and grief has nothing to do with them. Explain that your sadness and grief is because you miss their sibling, and that their sibling's death is very painful to you. Make sure your remaining children understand their importance and value to you. While going through grief, many parents have inadvertently isolated from their remaining children, damaging their relationship with them. It is so very important to pour yourself into your remaining relationships because they are still in need of your love. Be sure to let your remaining children know that they are important to you and that they bring you joy—they need to know that their sheer presence brings you joy and comfort. They may not understand how to help or communicate how they feel, so be sure to tell them that they are a part of the healing process in your family. Have them feel included.

When children go through grief, or watch a parent grieve, their world as they know it collapses. In addition to being sad, they may be confused, insecure, scared, angry, or unsure of what to expect. Please make your child's stability and security a top priority. Explain what has happened in their terms so they are able to comprehend their new reality. When going through grief, you have the powerful opportunity of being a positive role model for your children. They are looking to you as their primary example of how to handle life, grief, loss, feelings, and life challenges. Assure them that you love them, and reassure them that your family is going to get through this sad time. Allow them to know that life eventually will be stable again—and that life truly is still a gift.

I was young when my dad died, and it was so confusing to see my dad in his casket, while I tried to comprehend where Heaven was . . . and why He had to go there. I remember my older sister saying, "Shh! Dad is asleep." I knew that he was not asleep, I understood that he was dead, *but I thought being dead was temporary.* I thought that he would eventually come back. I remember how I would call his work phone number, and listen to his voice message over and over again, then go hide somewhere to cry. I remember my mom crying a lot and my Nana coming to stay with us to help our family through our time of grief. It was so comforting to have my Nana, aunts, and uncles there for all of us during that transitioning time. We were already close, but by helping each other through grief, our bonds became stronger. Four years after my dad died, my Nana died unexpectedly too. My entire world fell out from under me again. My dad dying, and my favorite grandmother dying shortly after, made an impression on me . . . and threw me into a state of insecurity. I began having horrible nightmares and the nightmares would plague me into my young adult years as well. If your child is struggling with insecurity or fear, memorizing scripture with your child can be very beneficial during grief. When they are fearful, assure them of God's protection and love. A meaningful verse that addresses fear is 2 Timothy 1:7, *"For God has not given us a spirit of fear, but of power and of love and of a sound mind."* (NKJV) I credit memorizing scripture in overcoming my constant nightmares and insecurity. In every area of my life, scripture has offered the best instruction and help for every situation. 2 Timothy 3:16, *"All Scripture is God-breathed and is useful for teaching, rebuking, correcting and training in righteousness"* (NIV) Allow God's Word to positively change your life and heal your grief. Read scripture with your family, talk about God's Word with them, and allow God's Word to help you and your family through the roller coaster ride of grief.

It is so important to communicate with your child, to fill in the gaps of understanding, and to make sure your child transitions into a healthy way of grieving. Please do not use clichés such as, "God needed Mommy" or "Heaven needed another angel," because that confuses children. They begin to think of God as somebody that stole their parent, or worse, caused their parent's death. Instead, be factual while compassionately talking to your child. It is helpful to describe Heaven and to tell your child that Heaven is where their loved one now resides. Be sure to let them know that God is sad when they are sad, and He understands their pain. When helping a child through grief, let them know that you are there to answer any questions they might have and that they can talk to you, or God, at anytime. I am truly thankful that my mom, and also her new husband, allowed me the freedom to talk about my dad . . . and my feelings about his death . . . while growing up. My mom, new dad, and I had many conversations about my first dad when they would take me to visit my first dad's grave.

Be sure to allow your child to talk openly about their deceased loved one if they desire to do so. To cut off communication about a child's deceased parent is to cut off an important piece of that child's identity and heart. You will strip them of part of their identity if you act as though their deceased parent never existed. Validate, honor, and value their thoughts and feelings. If your child was close to the deceased parent's family at the time of death, be sure to maintain a close relationship with them post-death. I am very grateful that my mom and her new husband ensured that I maintained a close relationship with my first dad's family throughout the years. When I later fully realized (as an adult) how well my mom and new dad honored my grief and my first dad's memory, I had an even deeper respect for them for truly caring about my heart and wellbeing. There are many parents that remarry and then neglect or write off the deceased spouse's family. I truly respect my dad for embracing my first dad's family as his own. I imagine it was bittersweet for my new dad to hear us talking about my first dad throughout the years—I have the highest regards for my new dad's decision of putting our emotional wellbeing and best interests above his own.

I have found throughout the years that everybody processes their grief very uniquely. My mom was wise to not only allow my siblings and me the freedom to talk about our dad; she was wise in understanding that we each dealt with our grief in our own way. Each child needs to be comforted individually and uniquely throughout their grief process. Approach them from their uniqueness. Grieving styles are different for everyone and children grieve uniquely as well. By honoring your child's grief, and the memory of your child's deceased parent, you are truly honoring your child. You are teaching them to value and honor the person that contributed in giving them life. Each child will process grief differently. Some will cry, some may not. Some may want to talk about their feelings, while others might not. Some will want to grieve openly, while some will prefer to grieve privately. Just like adults, children need the freedom to grieve in their very own unique way. Ask God to grant you the wisdom to understand how you can help your child to heal from their grief.

Talking with your child about their feelings and their grief, at an age appropriate level, is not only beneficial—it's needed. I remember after my Nana died, I felt a lot of unnecessary guilt. My Nana and I shared a very close relationship—and a sweet tooth. I had made her some chocolate pudding to surprise her the morning she was hospitalized, and I had also talked her into making peach cobbler earlier that day. When she was hospitalized, I overheard her nurse say that she wasn't doing well because of her sugar diabetes. I had no idea what diabetes was, but I knew that she had eaten sugary treats with me the day she was admitted to the hospital. When she died, I felt responsible for her death. I had thought, in my limited child's mind, that eating sugar had killed her. I didn't understand the medical terminology of diabetes, and

I didn't realize that she died in surgery from complications. You may want to ask your child age appropriate questions to better understand how they feel, and you definitely want to assure them that nothing is their fault. When I understood what diabetes was years later, I was so relieved to know that the pudding I had surprised my Nana with had nothing to do with her death.

Once you open up the communication lines with your child, think of a special activity that you can enjoy together. There are many activities that you can do with your child. Plan a special day of going to see a movie, going to the zoo, having a picnic at the park, or making a scrapbook. If you choose to create a scrapbook, gather pictures of you, your child and their siblings, their deceased parent, extended family of yours and your deceased spouse's family, and extended family. If you or their deceased parent ever gave them any cards or keepsakes, include those in the album too. Other ideas you could do is to make a charitable contribution in their deceased parent's name. You may want to give your child a picture frame with their loved one's photo in it to place in their room. At zoos and theme parks, occasionally they have bricks you can have engraved with a loved one's name that are displayed. You may want to take your child to pick out a tree to plant in your loved one's honor. There are opportunities online to purchase a real star and name it . . . you may want to name a star in their deceased parent's honor. You can also research opportunities online of how to honor a loved one, and then do what is most memorable and comfortable for your family. There are many opportunities and ideas to honor a loved one's memory—the goal is for your child to feel the freedom to talk to you about their grief, to feel comfortable in honoring their deceased parent, and to develop a closer bond to you and remaining family members. The memory album you create with your child, or any other act of remembrance, will be treasured for years to come. They will honor you for genuinely caring about their grief, their emotional security, and their feelings.

How can a stepparent help their stepchild through loss? Many times, a stepparent is unsure of where they fit into their stepchild's grieving process. If you are the stepparent of a child whose parent has passed away, you have a wonderful opportunity to help your stepchild through their grief. Allow your stepchild to talk freely about their grief and their deceased parent, and allow them to talk about their feelings associated with their loss. When they later realize how you honored their heart, grief, and their deceased parent's memory, your child will honor and respect you for truly caring about their ultimate wellbeing. If you have blended into your stepchild's family after the death of their parent, do not feel as though your stepchild is rejecting or betraying you by remembering their deceased parent, for that is not their intention—their parent is a part of who they are. They will always love and remember their parent in the depths of their heart. Even though they continue to remember and love their deceased parent, they have a strong ability to have a close relationship and bond with you as well. Allowing your stepchild to properly grieve in a healthy way shows your stepchild that you value and validate their feelings. If you are concerned that your stepchild's love for their deceased parent (or their deceased parent's family) will lessen their love for you, there is no need for concern. A child is more than capable of loving and caring about multiple family members, so never feel as though you're in a competition or second-rate. You have a blessed opportunity of being a great role model and friend to your stepchild as you help them through their grief. Realize that grief is sometimes very difficult to process, so do not be surprised if your stepchild goes through a myriad of emotions. Even in your best attempts to be loving and helpful, a stepchild may wrongly react to you—be patient with your stepchild, knowing that their reaction is formed out of frustration due to being in great emotional pain. Be a trustworthy and dependable friend to your stepchild during this heartbreaking time in their life. It may be tempting to try to take over as "the parent," but that will usually lead to reaction and may harm your relationship in the long run. A stepparent will usually get a reaction from their stepchild if the child (rightfully or wrongfully) perceives that the stepparent is trying to replace their deceased parent. Explain to your stepchild that their deceased parent will always be their parent—explain that you are not trying to replace their parent—communicate to them that you want to be an accepted and welcomed addition to their family. Focus on creating a genuinely close relationship with your stepchild, for you have the ability to develop a solid relationship with them that is filled with mutual love, respect, and honor. They will begin to welcome any encouragement, love, and support that you can offer as they sense your genuine love and concern for them. Communication (and honor) is key. You may want to research blended families and look for opportunities and ways to build unity into your blended family. The goal is for your stepchild: to feel the freedom to talk to you and your spouse about their feelings, to grieve in the healthiest and most honorable way possible, to feel the freedom to love and honor their deceased parent, to understand the importance of honoring a deceased loved one's memory, to feel secure as a result of blending *all* of their loved family members together (parent, stepparent, siblings, parent's family, deceased parent's family, stepparent's family) and to develop a loving relationship and close bond to you. I truly believe that every child has the capacity to love and honor both their deceased parent *and* stepparent . . . it doesn't have to be either or. I consider *both* my birth dad and my second dad my "real" parents. Depending on how much you honor your stepchild's grief and their deceased parent, your stepchild will either respect you for genuinely caring about their grief, their emotional security, and their feelings . . . or they will eventually detach from you if they sense any lack of genuine love or concern for them. You have such a wonderful opportunity to pour into your stepchild and new spouse's life, learning how to love like Christ, as you begin to build your new family unit. If God has called you to be a stepparent . . . what an amazing calling He has entrusted to you! God will be faithful to equip you to meet your stepchild's emotional needs as you go to God for His wisdom, love, and support. God is the author and creator of family and He desires for families to develop unity, love, and close bonds. I am so grateful for my second dad and our relationship that has been developed throughout the years. My second dad's ability and decision to truly honor my feelings, my first dad's memory, and my first dad's family made all the difference in the world in my ability to trust, respect, accept, and love him.

As a stepparent, you have a God-given opportunity to honor your stepchild's deceased parent's memory by being kind and loving towards your stepchild's extended family (the parents, grandparents, siblings, nieces, nephews, and other family members of the deceased parent). Please remember that the deceased parent's entire family is also going through a lot of pain . . . and they may feel unsure as to where they will fit into your newly blended family. Be compassionate, thoughtful, and sensitive to your stepchild's extended family. Include them in your lives, as well as special occasions and holidays. You will find that as you accept, love, and include them . . . they should accept, love, and include you as well. It is in your stepchild's best interests to continue being close to family members that they were close to before their parent's death. Encourage these important relationships by ensuring quality time together through combined family activities, special occasions, birthday celebrations, and holiday dinners. A stepparent (together with their spouse) certainly has their work cut out for them in developing family harmony and unity, but the eventual rewards of respect and honor will make all of their efforts well worth it. As you seek God, may He bless you, your stepchild, spouse, and your blended families with unity, love, and genuine harmony throughout the years.

Creating an environment of security and stability will be beneficial to your child now and also in the years to come. When my dad died, a great portion of my security was destroyed and I always felt as though a part of me was missing. Whenever a child loses a parent while growing up, I really believe that there is an internal feeling of void and insecurity due to not having the ability to thoroughly process their loss. Looking back now as an adult, I can clearly see there were decisions I subconsciously made due to losing my dad and not understanding how to grieve my dad's death. Seeking to understand my feeling that something was missing, and trying to understand the reasons behind my attempts to fill that void in my life, I made the wise decision to grieve my dad's death. I still have several memories of my dad that I treasure, but it would have been great to have had the opportunity to have known him better. I am really grateful that I took the time to clearly see what losing my dad meant to me. After thoroughly grieving his death, and going to God with my grief, I had a renewed sense of security and peace. If you have gone through the death of a parent, please know that God deeply cares about your grief and loss. A verse that is very meaningful is Psalm 68:5, *"A father of the fatherless and a champion of widows is God in His holy dwelling."* (HCSB) When you have lost a parent or a spouse, God is faithful to fill the void in your hurting heart as you seek His love, healing, and comfort. It may take time, but He is faithful and true to His Word.

There are so many rich lessons you can learn from grief as a family. Grief has taught our family selflessness, deference, loyalty, and to deeply care about each and every family member. Our family is very close because we went through my dad, sister, grandparents, uncles, and other family members deaths together. When my sister went through the deaths of two different fiancés, we all gathered together to shower her with love, support, encouragement, and hope. Grief has created a very strong bond in our family that we would not have if we had never gone through loss. I cannot stress this point strongly enough: be there for your family, and offer them encouragement, love, support, and hope. Their world falls apart when grieving. Be extra sensitive, loving, compassionate, and understanding during their grief.

Nothing has helped me in my healing process relationally as much as my family and friends. It is truly incredible how God places families together, and forms friendships that He knew we would need during our times of bereavement. Having a support system that I can go to for love, encouragement, and support is priceless to me. I value all of my family and good friends so very much. They truly have helped me more than they will ever realize. As I have gone through the loneliness of grief, my family has been one of God's greatest gifts to me. Whether you have a family or a group of friends that are helping you through your grief, thank God for supplying you with familial encouragement. Psalm 68:6, *"God sets the lonely in families . . . "* (NIV)

Take all the time you need to process the reality of your loss. It may take awhile for it all to completely soak in. After the initial shock, it's as though God places a numbing veil around you. For the first couple of days, and maybe even weeks after a loved one dies, reality becomes a blur. After the funeral, when everybody else goes on with life as usual, that is when the veil lifts and the pain becomes all too real. At that point, the excuses, busyness, and wishing away reality quickly wears off. It is then you realize your genuine need for God, family, friends, and community. You do not have to go through your grief alone. Ask God to provide you with the family, friends, and community you'll need to overcome your grief.

Take time today to thank God for the people in your life that are helping you through your grief and for those who have taken the time to encourage you. As a gift back to God to show Him your gratefulness, look for ways you can be a blessing and encouragement in the lives of others. After my sister's fiancé died, a generous woman allowed my sister to stay at her lake house for an extended weekend of solitude. My sister invited our parents, my son, and me to stay with her. That weekend we were able to offer my sister compassion and encouragement. Later in the weekend, our oldest sister and her family came up for the day. This was a really great time of remembrance and healing for our family as we reflected on her fiancé's life. I am so grateful to the generous lady that allowed my sister to use her lake house because it allowed our family to "get away" together—it also allowed me to video my oldest sister and her daughters that weekend. It was a crisp Fall day at the lake house and there were tons of leaves all over the ground. My sister played in the leaves with her daughters and my son while I video recorded them having fun. That video footage is so treasured because it was only a few weeks later that my sister suddenly died. I will forever be grateful for this lady that showed my sister kindness. She is a wonderful example of looking for a way to be a blessing in the lives of those going through grief—she is an excellent example of community. *use my life, Lord*

Some of the most beautiful benefits of grief, loss, and life challenges are learning through your grief, being encouraged, and being an encouragement in the lives of others. If you know of a family member or friend who is facing a struggle, or a loss that you have faced, look for ways to encourage them during their grief process. That is what God designed every human being for: to love Him and others through Him. You have the blessed ability to assist, encourage, and help others who are going through a similar loss. If you have experienced a loved one dying, you can genuinely empathize and help them through their grief. If you have gone through the heartbreak of abandonment, divorce, or infidelity, you have a powerful ability to help others through their relational crises. If you have been through illness, you know firsthand how to encourage others going through a medical hardship. It is God's desire for people to encourage and help others through their trials. 2 Corinthians 1:3-4, *"All praise to God, the Father of our Lord Jesus Christ. God is our merciful Father and the source of all comfort. He comforts us in all our troubles so that we can comfort others. When they are troubled, we will be able to give them the same comfort God has given us."* (NLT) As you encourage and help others through their grief, please remember to respect a person's confidentiality. When someone thinks so highly of you that they entrust their heart into your hands by confiding in you, that is a treasure. Don't betray their trust by abusing that precious gift. I once confided in a friend about a particular grief experience and I really liked her viewpoint of keeping a confidence. She said, "I won't tell your story, it's not *my* story to tell."

God desires for His children to look outside their own lives and interests. When we look outside of ourselves, we then are able to be sensitive to the needs and interests of others. As we receive encouragement, comfort, and compassion from Christ, He desires for us to pay it forward. Philippians 2:1-4, *"Therefore if you have any encouragement from being united with Christ, if any comfort from his love, if any common sharing in the Spirit, if any tenderness and compassion, then make my joy complete by being like-minded, having the same love, being one in spirit and of one mind. Do nothing out of selfish ambition or vain conceit. Rather, in humility value others above yourselves, not looking to your own interests but each of you to the interests of the others."* (NIV) God calls us to minister and encourage others through every season of our lives—even in the midst of grief. Look for ways and opportunities where God can use you to be a source of encouragement to others. God delights in using our talents and spiritual gifts for His glory, plans, and purpose. He also is able to use our heartaches and loss for His glory and purposes as well. Ask God to show you how you can best use your God-given talents, spiritual gifts, as well as your grief and loss experiences, to build relationships for His glory. Build relationships so that you can encourage and minister to others while sharing the Reason for your hope.

The relationships and communities that God blesses us with are such an incredible gift. Let each of us thank God for these great gifts, and ask Him how we can be a blessing to others during times of grief, loss, and the challenges of life.

"Heavenly Father, thank you for each of the relationships that you have blessed me with. I ask and trust You to bring the relationships I need into my life to truly heal. Bless my life with community. Thank you for every word of encouragement, act of love, and emotional support that I have received from You and others You have placed in my life. Lord, may all my relationships honor and glorify You. Pour Your perfect peace, love, and hope into my heart and life and bring healing as only You can. As you bring my heart encouragement, I pray that You will give me a sensitive heart towards others during times of grief. Teach me to love like You love and give me the grace to comfort others. Lord, help me to truly be there for my family and protect our hearts. Help us through our grief and struggles, and give us the grace to be compassionate, loving, and understanding with each other. Give us the grace to honor

and respect each other's grief process. Lord, I love You, thank You for being the ultimate example of community, and for guiding and directing me and my family through life. Thank You for being my truest, most faithful Friend. In Jesus Name I pray, Amen"

3 Oxygens

1. Communicate with your family about grief, especially if there are children involved. Support, love, and honor each other through grief. Take time to encourage each other and spend time together.

2. Use your God-given talents, spiritual gifts, as well as your grief and loss experiences, to encourage and bless others. Allow God to guide you in building relationships and community with others.

3. Make a memory book of your loved one that is filled with photos, cards, and keepsakes. Consider making a charitable contribution in your loved one's name or memory.

Help for Family Conflict During Grief~

Sometimes, when there is a death in the family, there is immediate conflict . . . or conflict may arise in the future . . . due to the family dynamics changing. I have witnessed many families suffer from disharmony due to not understanding (or being unprepared for) the challenges and aftermath of a loved one dying. Even if a family goes through the process of getting their breath back after life has knocked it out of them, there are challenges that can knock their breath right back out of them. I've witnessed families who have destroyed each other due to playing the blame game after a loved one's death. I've seen families disintegrate due to financial and inheritance issues. I've also seen families be thoroughly torn apart when a parent remarries, then the parent or their new spouse causes conflict out of a lack of Christ-like love and concern for the children or the deceased parent's extended family. Sometimes, families fall apart due to not respecting each other's grief process. After the death of a child, an illness, or other loss, I have known of spouses confiding in and finding comfort in someone of the opposite sex—and as a result, an affair blooms, destroying both families involved.

When loss takes place, all involved are catapulted into unfamiliar territory which paves the way for families to uncharacteristically not think or act right. Regardless of how poorly families may behave in response to their grief, I sincerely believe that God has the power to maintain, or bring about, family unity when all involved are willing to: set aside personal preferences, forgive, be a peacemaker, and obey God's Word.

God desires for families to get along—He does not want anyone to be put in the middle—and it is best for all remaining family members to get along with, and show deference to, *every* member of their family: parents, siblings, grandparents, aunts, uncles, cousins, etc. If family conflict arises after the death of a loved one, all involved need to work the issues out amicably and implement respect, honor, and obeying God's principles of loving others. It is important for everyone involved to have a spirit of unity, regardless of feelings and personal preferences. Feelings need to be set aside, for it is not fair for a family to go through contention or further loss due to one or all not acting in good character. All have the God-given opportunity to encourage and minister to each other during grief. You can bring glory to God by being a peacemaker and ensuring unity: Matthew 5:9, *"Blessed are the peacemakers, for they will be called children of God."* (NIV) If this is a challenge, everybody needs to remember that there is an opportunity to resolve conflict, and more importantly, to honor God and family.

During times of conflict, it will take work for all family members involved to live honorably in showing deference, but it *can* be accomplished. Everyone involved needs to display maturity by choosing to be kind, considerate, flexible, and to ultimately do what is right in God's eyes. It helps to remember Ephesians 4:2-3, *"Be completely humble and gentle; be patient, bearing with one another in love. Make every effort to keep the unity of the Spirit through the bond of peace."* (NIV) Any act of truly caring about another's wellbeing and the integrity of family during times of conflict will eventually be rewarded by God for being honorable in times of bereavement. God will truly reward a person's efforts of being a peacemaker through His promise in James 3:18, *"Peacemakers who sow in peace reap a harvest of righteousness."* (NIV)

Yes, it can be difficult when achieving family harmony, especially through times of grief, but it can be accomplished if everyone is willing to put God first. When we only look at what we want, without using deference towards others, that is when conflicts begin. Proverbs 13:10 says, *"Only by pride cometh contention: but with the well advised is wisdom."* (KJV) As each family member removes their pride, seeks God's wisdom, and receives godly counsel, everyone then has the freedom and ability to look at conflict through the eyes of Christ. 2 Chronicles 7:14 is a verse that reveals God's healing power, *"If my people, who are called by my name, will humble themselves and pray and seek my face and turn from their wicked ways, then I will hear from heaven, and I will forgive their sin and will heal their land."* (NIV) Pray to God for wisdom in how to handle situations of conflict and contention, remove all pride, and be honorable in all you do. If conflict remains, you may want to seek pastoral care or counsel with a neutral third party.

Additional Help For Families Who Remarry~

When a remaining parent gets remarried, it is important for the remaining parent and their new potential spouse to have an important discussion before going into marriage. Discussing important topics before marriage can prevent a lot of stress for the new couple in the future.

Sometimes, a remaining parent, or a new stepparent, will have the unrealistic expectation that their newly formed family will only consist of their two families being joined. When a remarriage takes place, there is a joining of not only two families, but actually *three* families: the remaining parent's family, the stepparent's family, *and the deceased parent's family.* It is very important to realize that just because a deceased parent died, it does not mean that the deceased parent's extended family died along with them.

A caring loving family member on the deceased parent's side of the family should not be cut off, sabotaged, or kept from a child's life.

On the other hand, it is not right for the deceased parent's family to unfairly sabotage a child's relationship with their new stepparent or the stepparent's family.

A caring parent, stepparent, and both their extended families will support and encourage the child's relationships with the deceased parent's family (the deceased parent's parents, siblings, grandparents, aunts, uncles, cousins, etc.) and the deceased parent's family should encourage and support the newly formed family of the remaining parent and their new spouse.

Sometimes, a deceased parent's family may feel as though the new stepparent, or the stepparent's family, is replacing them or taking their God-given family away from them...and the new stepparent and stepparent's family may feel as though the child will not bond with them if the child is frequently around the deceased parent's family.

Children desire for their loved ones to get along, and it is best for children to get along with *every* member of their family: parents, stepparents, siblings, grandparents, aunts, uncles, cousins, stepfamilies, etc. Allowing already established family members to continue to be in a child's life, and to encourage a child's relationship with their new stepfamily, is not only fair...it's right.

It may be easy for a stepparent, and the stepparent's extended family, to welcome the deceased parent's family into their lives...or it may be a challenge. On the other hand, it may be easy for the deceased parent's family to accept the new stepparent, or it may be a challenge. Through all scenarios, honoring God and the best interests of the child is what should come first.

It is in the child's best interests to continue enjoying activities, special occasions, birthdays, and holiday dinners with their remaining parent's family, as well as the deceased parent's family, if that has been the norm for the child. Please do not add heartache to the deceased parent's family (and the child) by not allowing the child's participation in holiday dinners, family activities, family portraits, and special occasions. The deceased parent's family has already been through heartbreaking grief due to the death of their loved one, don't add further loss or compound their grief by being unthoughtful, insensitive, or difficult. Likewise, it is not fair for the deceased parent's family to not accept a child's new stepparent just because they are not the original parent. Please look at the new stepparent as a unique God-created individual and as a new addition to your family. The stepparent is not to be expected to be a replacement of (nor replica for) the deceased parent.

Another topic the remaining parent and potential stepparent will need to discuss is holiday dinners. How will they handle holidays, and where will they spend them? Please have compassion for the deceased parent's family. They did not *choose* for the deceased parent to die. Holidays are hard enough not having their loved one there—please don't prevent their loved one's children from attending occasional holiday dinners. Consider alternating Easter, Thanksgiving, and Christmas dinners with the three families involved, rotating turns and holidays. Another option is for the families to have holiday dinners a week before the real holiday if it's not their turn in the rotation.

It is important for everyone involved to work together and to have a spirit of unity, regardless of feelings and preferences. Feelings need to be set aside, it is not fair to have a child go through contention or further loss due to the adults creating issues with one another. All have the grand opportunity to encourage ALL family relationships. It may be a challenge to the adults, but children desire for their families to be unified. If this is a challenge, everybody needs to make the mature decision to bring honor ultimately to God. It may be easier for the adults to have separate get togethers, parties, and holiday dinners, but it ultimately may be at the expense of the child's security. Even if there isn't conflict, a child may perceive it as being conflict if the families begin hosting separate birthday parties and holiday dinners...having one party for the stepfamily's side, then having a separate party for the deceased family's side...after the child has been accustomed to the families celebrating together.

It is important to blend all three families into the child's life. When a child feels like there is conflict, they will begin to try to please all sets of families, and even degrade their own conscience to do so. Matthew 6:24 is a verse that speaks of loyalty to God over money, but I believe this verse is useful guidance for family conflict as well, *"No one can serve two masters. Either you will hate the one and love the other, or you will be devoted to the one and despise the other..."* (NIV) It will take work for all families involved to live honorably in showing deference, but it *can* be accomplished. Nobody chooses for a grief experience to take place, but since it has, everyone involved needs to be mature, accepting of one another, and show deference. All involved must work together to do what is truly best for the child. After the child becomes an adult, whoever truly cared about the child's wellbeing will eventually be appreciated, honored, and highly respected for caring about the child's heart, and for being honorable in times of grief. They will clearly see, appreciate, and understand each family's sacrifice and love for them as they grow older...especially when they have children of their own. The three families involved have a high responsibility: they are all a blueprint of teaching a child what family truly is, and they are forming a child's opinions about family, conflict, harmony, and God.

It is very important for the remaining spouse and the new stepparent to spend time together with just them and their children. All families involved will need to realize that the newly formed family is adjusting to being a family, balancing responsibilities and schedules, and learning how to live together in harmony. They will need to find what works for them so they can create a marriage and home life that achieves God's goals for their family. They will probably do things differently than before because the dynamics of their home has now changed. Offer them any encouragement and support that God leads you to.

These are topics the remaining parent and their new potential spouse will need to consider to prevent future conflict and heartache for all families involved.

Yes, it can be challenging to blend three families, especially through times of grief, but it can be accomplished if everyone is willing to put God first. He created each family with who He desired to be in the family unit, so if someone goes against that, they're attempting to alter God's ultimate plan. Pray to God for wisdom in how to handle situations of conflict, remove all pride, and be honorable in all you do. If conflict is present (or continues), you may want to seek pastoral care or counsel with a neutral third party.

CHAPTER 8

~

The Oxygen
of Time

When someone you deeply love dies, or you experience a crushing loss, it becomes hard to get through the day. The world feels as though it has stopped. Time seems to stand still, and it becomes an excruciating chore to take the necessary steps to go through the daily routine of responsibilities, as well as to thoroughly grieve. I know when I go through times of grief, I am tempted to try to find any and every way I possibly can to shorten the duration of the pain I am experiencing. Difficult situations hurt and most people are desperate to feel better as quick as possible—but that isn't the best method of handling grief in the long run. In your grief recovery, don't be surprised if you find yourself wanting to get through the pain as soon as possible, but I appeal to you to not put a time limit on your grief. Grief takes time and has to play out on its own. Be patient with yourself and your grief process. I can't say it enough: grief, loss, and life challenges are to be embraced—for there are lessons to be learned that are so valuable. You simply cannot learn these valuable lessons any other way. There are going to be days when everything will seem to go well, and there are going to be days when you seriously will want to crawl back into bed and never get out. There will be all sorts of feelings, all sorts of days, because you are grieving on so many different levels. Do not shortchange yourself and your loved ones around you by attempting to shorten or control your grief. It takes time. On the days you feel you simply cannot go on, run to God. He is there waiting for you to run to Him for comfort and strength. Through my times of grief, I have found that God has a very specific timetable and season for everything. Seasons will come and seasons will go, so do not lose heart. God has a purpose and a specific time for everything under the heavens. Your life may currently be filled with heartache—but a new season is to come.

Ecclesiastes 3:1-8,

"To every thing there is a season, and a time to every purpose under the heaven:
A time to be born, and a time to die;
a time to plant, and a time to pluck up that which is planted;
A time to kill, and a time to heal;
a time to break down, and a time to build up;
A time to weep, and a time to laugh;
a time to mourn, and a time to dance;
A time to cast away stones, and a time to gather stones together;
a time to embrace, and a time to refrain from embracing;
A time to get, and a time to lose;
a time to keep, and a time to cast away;
A time to rend, and a time to sew;
a time to keep silence, and a time to speak;
A time to love, and a time to hate;
a time of war, and a time of peace." (KJV)

Something the Lord continually repeats to me in times of bereavement is this: although grief is horribly painful, grief and God's timetable for grief is to be accepted and not hurried. Embracing God's times of grief for my life, and seeking His heart, has allowed me to grow in my relationship with Him, in a way that I never could have experienced had my life been void of pain. As I have run to Him with my pain, He has been so faithful to rebuild and heal my heart in His perfect timing—He never quits. God will be there throughout your entire grief experience, from the beginning to the end. Hebrews 13:5 says, *"Never will I leave you; never will I forsake you."* (NIV) You can depend on God to be there. As you run to Him, expect to have your relationship with Him beautifully deepen over time.

Being patient while going through grief is challenging at times. There have been times that I resented my grief to its very core. I had to ask God for the patience to wait for His perfect timing. Take the necessary time you need to thoroughly go through your grief with God by your side. I encourage you today to make the commitment to not rush through your grief, but instead take the time to see exactly what God's purpose and plan is for the pain you are experiencing. Pour your heart out to God and ask Him to meet you in the depths of your pain. Ask Him to guide and direct you through your grief in His perfect timing. You will find that He is the only one who can truly offer you longterm healing. Set aside some time to be upfront and real with God. If you're discouraged or upset, tell Him. If you feel as though you are dying from heartache, share that with Him. In your times of being severely heartbroken, share your deepest feelings and thoughts with Him. Remove the timetables you have placed on God, or yourself, to remove your pain. It is so easy to feel emotionally and spiritually drained, physically worn out, and depressed as if there is no hope of ever feeling better. Cry out to God for His help to get you through the day—take it one day at a time. You may even have to ask Him to help you get through the pain hour by hour. He knows exactly where you are in your grief process. Pour your heart out to Him and ask Him to comfort your heart while healing your soul. You will find that there is hope, comfort, and love in Him unlike anything you have experienced. Throughout life, you have the opportunity to develop a strong friendship with God—the goal is not to have a relationship with God only through our times of grief; the goal is to develop an ongoing relationship with God into eternity.

During your grief experience, I will warn you that you may not think clearly for awhile so please take the proper time to heal. After loss, most people go through a period of time of sheer shock . . . and nobody thinks straight while going through shock. Anytime you go through loss, it is a wise idea to hold off on making any major decisions for at least a year. You probably are not going to be in your right mind, so give yourself a year to get your thoughts and your heart lined up so you can make the wisest decisions.

Don't Jump into a relationship

If your loss was a relational loss, don't jump into dating or remarrying prematurely. If your spouse has died, it may be tempting to try to compensate for your loss through finding a companion. Life is excruciatingly painful and lonely after your mate has died. There is an intense void that renders you completely heartbroken. I know of many people who prematurely dated, or remarried, and further compounded their grief after they began thinking straight again. It is not fair to the new partner to be a replacement of a deceased spouse, especially since they will be placed into the unfair position of likely never being able to measure up to the one who has passed away. Each person is deserving of finding love or being loved for the right reasons, so please do not rush into remarriage with wrong motives. It takes time to genuinely fall in love, to truly get to know somebody, so don't be rash in your judgment when it comes to marriage.

Grasping your emotions and the depth of your loss takes time. Be patient with yourself and do not feel as though you need to rush any part of your life. You just had the breath knocked out of you and it will take time to get your breath back. When a loved one dies, there are so many complex emotions and situations you will have to face. You will need time to come to terms with your loss and your feelings will fluctuate. Something my mom chose to do after my dad died was to leave all of his belongings exactly the way he left them for an entire year. You may want to leave everything exactly how it was the day of your loss until you are able to truly understand the complexity of your loss. It is wise to wait an entire year because how you feel in your fresh grief and shock cannot be trusted. Many people clean out closets or clean rooms in their house only to regret it later on. In the first weeks after a loved one has died, don't be surprised if it becomes painful to look at their belongings or their photos. You may feel tempted to remove these items in a moment of pain, but realize you will not always feel the same intensity of grief as you feel in the initial weeks of your grief. Sometimes well meaning people will give you advice on what you should do, and sometimes they will start to clean your house or a loved one's bedroom without asking. Make your precise wishes known to leave everything as it is for a year. You don't want to add on to your grief by having to deal with regrets later on. Please know that it isn't wrong to remove belongings after thoroughly grieving your loved one. After coming to terms with your loss and grief, you might choose to continue leaving everything as is, you may choose to remove belongings, or you may allow other family members or friends to go through your loved one's belongings so they can have a keepsake of your loved one's life. None of these choices are wrong, just be sure to fully understand your decisions before doing anything.

Some people want to be around their loved one's belongings or their photographs. It brings great comfort to them and makes them feel closer to their loved one throughout their grief process. There is nothing wrong with wearing a loved one's clothing, smelling their pillow, wanting to hold personal items like a blanket, stuffed animal, or coat, or being comforted through photos and home videos. After my sister's fiancé died, she wore his sweatshirts for several months. After my sister's death, I watched home videos and looked at photos often. I also made a scrapbook filled with photos and the cards that she had given me. When I miss my sister, I occasionally look through my scrapbook or watch home videos. Sometimes I simply ask God to tell her hello for me and that I love and miss her.

It is important to take whatever time you need to grieve and to do whatever helps you to thoroughly grieve. Grief is like a crossword puzzle—you have to be the one to figure it out in your individual time frame. You might want to enlist the help of others, or you might want to work your grief out by yourself. The important thing is to grieve in a way that is in your time, in a way that is comfortable to you. I cannot stress enough: there is not one specific correct way to grieve. You will know when the time is right to move forward. When I say move forward, I am not suggesting forgetting your loved one, or that your grief will suddenly completely end. Moving forward is simply building a new life when you are healthy enough to do so. It takes time to mend a broken heart, and time and strength to rebuild your life from the ground up. If you become stuck in your grief, you may need additional help from a pastor or counselor to move forward and that is okay. Honorably do whatever you need to do to become healthy enough to enjoy life once again.

Although grief never completely ends, it becomes much more bearable over time. You will eventually have the ability to love and enjoy life once again. Grief is a part of your life forever once you experience it, for the memory of your loved one, and the valuable lessons you learn stay deep within your soul. It eventually becomes dulled, but it can be awakened at any time. I have always thought that grief is much like a tattoo. When going through the first stages of grief, it pierces and breaks your heart, leaving an indelible mark. After a while, it begins to scab over, but even the smallest happening can rip the scab off completely, setting the healing process back. After the the scab eventually heals, there is a permanent tattoo on your heart. There will be good days, bad days, as well as in-between days. There will eventually be long periods of time after healing where everything will be going wonderful, *but* be warned that grief can resurface from time to time. Many years after my sister's death, my grief resurfaced during a year of special celebrations. My sister's oldest daughter became engaged and got married, her middle daughter had a baby, and her youngest daughter graduated high school all in the same year. I grieved that my sister had to miss these special milestones with her daughters. My sister was an excellent mother who loved and adored her girls, and I know if she were alive, she would have loved being a part of these special occasions. She would have delighted in planning her oldest daughter's wedding with her, going shopping to help her find a wedding dress, and I know she would have sentimentally cried when she saw her daughter in her wedding dress for the first time. My sister would have loved planning the celebrations and parties for these special occasions, and would have absolutely loved celebrating the birth of her first grandchild. She adored her daughters in life and I was very sad she didn't get to experience these wonderful special occasions with them. I was surprised by my grief resurfacing the way it did with each of these occasions. I found out firsthand that going through grief is definitely never a cut-and-dry experience with a cut-and-dry timetable. It is woven throughout our lives, in the tapestry of our hearts—it is our heart's way of remembering our loved one always.

It's very important to realize that God's timing is not our timing. Sometimes God will delight you by answering quickly . . . while other times, His timing will not seem quick enough. God is not looking at our situation from our limited worldly point of view or our earthly timetable—He is looking at our lives from a heavenly point of view, an eternal perspective. In His wisdom, He knows exactly what it is going to take for each grieving heart to have the ability to truly live life once again, and He is faithful to be there every step of the way. No matter how long it takes, He will be there. There *is* hope when we submit our grief into God's hands. Proverbs 23:18, *"There is surely a future hope for you, and your hope will not be cut off."* (NIV)

When life doesn't go the way you planned and everything is totally chaotic, it can seem as though life happens in slow motion. Life will eventually catch up to a normal time pattern. Waiting for time to catch up, and taking the time to learn from the life experiences you are going through, is often very hard. How do you rebuild a broken heart and how do you go about rebuilding your life? How can you make the most of your time while going through grief? Self reflection, asking for God's help, and goal setting, while taking small baby steps of progress each and every day, is the key.

Using a baby as an analogy is what I'll use to illustrate my next points. A baby doesn't start off by running a marathon. It takes time, growth, practice, and sometimes falling down, but always getting back up. It starts with God creating the baby and planning out their days before one day is even lived. The baby is born, then after being nurtured begins raising it's head, rolling over, crawling, pulling it's self up, taking baby steps with someone holding the baby's hands, walking independently, growing up a little, and then being able to run. These steps can be a very useful guide for rebuilding your life and heart through grief. Realize that every step takes time.

There is much you can learn about grief recovery using a baby as an analogy:

1. Birth—When a baby is born, it is catapulted into an entirely different environment. Where there used to be comfort, predictability, warmth, and safety, the baby is startled by a stressful entrance into a world of a cold, sterile, new, and unknown territory. The same happens with grief, as birthing and grieving processes are very similar. After a baby is born, the baby is washed, then swaddled in a warm blanket. The baby is very dependent and vulnerable and needs help in adapting to their new existence. As a baby's primary caretaker is key to the child's survival and well being, God becomes the primary source of wrapping His warmth around His grieving child. He takes on the responsibility of the grieved one's survival and well being as they begin to understand how to live in their new reality of life.

2. Raising your head—After being nurtured and growing stronger, a baby then has more solid strength to begin looking up and connecting with those around them at a more intimate level. Look up to God, seek Him first in all you do. Realize that He is there at the beginning

of your grief experience and He will be with you to the end. After you gain some much needed strength through God nurturing you during the initial weeks of your grief, you will be strengthened to have a much deeper relationship with Him. You will find more and more strength each time you look up to Him to be your comforter, love, grace, and truest friend during your grief recovery.

3. Rolling over—So after going through deep grief, you figure out that life has lost all or most of its meaning. You start to wonder if this is what life will ever be. You start the process of realizing something has got to change because you can't go on with the way things are. You do not enjoy the way your grief is forcing you to live and feel. You begin to realize the need to "roll over." Rolling over is what it takes to gain a new perspective. Rolling over is making the decision to try a new approach to your grief recovery, to make things different, and eventually making your circumstances better.

4. Crawling—You begin to crawl through your grief recovery, struggling to understand life and tragedy. Crawling involves half getting up, admitting that something terrible has happened. It might have been something that you had control over or it may have been something that hit you like a ton of unexpected bricks that you had no control over whatsoever. Next, you actively take an inventory of what happened and try to think of ways to get to the place in life that you need to be. You begin to truly see that life can potentially be better. You start to realize that since you're still here, you want to have a better existence than the grief-filled one you are living. You see a possibility of a better life but you realize that you'll have to crawl to get to it.

5. Pulling oneself up—At this point, crawling through the struggles of your grief recovery isn't good enough. You realize that you're growing sick of the way things have been so you get to the point of almost defiantly saying, *"You know what? With God's help, I am going to pull myself up because it's frustrating to feel so helpless!"* You start to think, *"What and who can help me to make things different?"* You then come up with some sort of plan to call or meet with those who can help you through the process of healing and assist you in making things better. It may be a friend,

family member, pastor, psychologist, medical or health professional, or another source of help. You have finally come to the point of accepting responsibility for your well being and are now ready and willing to make it happen. Now that you have enlisted the help of others, you are now ready to "walk" with some help.

6. Baby steps with the help of others—You've finally come to the point of accepting help for your situation and realize that no one is an island. We each need others for our ultimate wellbeing to be a reality. With someone holding your hand, you'll be much less likely to fail. You may fall down . . . but someone is going to be there to help you get back up. There are going to be extremely hard days so be prepared. It is vital to find an outside source of encouragement, strength, and help. Again, I recommend finding someone that is well trusted and respected. Make sure that who you choose to help you is someone that has your best interests at heart. Choose a person that is willing to be there for the times you need somebody to hold you up as you learn to "walk" again by yourself. Be careful not to allow others to take advantage of you or your situation during times of grief. Seek God and ask Him to help you make the wisest decisions.

7. Walking independently—Now that you have had someone help you through your initial grief, you will now begin to transition into learning to heal independently with God's help. Like a small child, just because you have learned to walk doesn't mean that you won't occasionally want to be carried when times are rough. For the most part, you'll appreciate achieving more and more independence in walking by yourself with God. You don't see many older kids being carried by their parents anymore but you do see them walking alongside their parents when they need to talk or need some encouragement for life. You see them having a relationship with their parents and enjoying time with them. That is the illustration that I am trying to paint here for you. As you truly heal, God will be walking by your side. As you go to Him for advice or encouragement, He is faithful to guide and direct you. You have grown in your relationship with God, so enjoy His love. You now enjoy the freedom of a solid relationship with God. In the initial days of grief, most prayers are focused on pouring your heart

out to God. You will find over time that your prayers will become more focused on God and how He is working *in* you instead of *on* you. An amazing love relationship with God will be your reward for allowing Him to walk beside you, leading you through your grief.

8. Growing up a little—After walking independently, you are now in a stage for optimal growth. Growing up takes time . . . and the timeline of maturity will be different for every person. The more tragic the loss, the longer it may take to grow from the loss. At this point, you have come to see that: yes, something horrible has happened, and you have seen the need to make things better. You have seen that you need outside help and encouragement, and you have enlisted the help of those that can help to make your life of better quality. Listen to me when I make this statement: *None of the progress you have made will be lasting if you're not willing to grow in maturity and realize that life is not always fair.* I say this because without understanding the fact that really bad things sometimes happen to really good people, you'll play the blame game, or drown in self-pity or bitterness, until it slowly destroys your life. Even after thoroughly grieving, grief can continually keep you captive for as long as you allow it, until you choose to look at heartbreaking situations through eyes of maturity. Viewing loss with eyes of maturity is difficult to do, especially when you feel you have been wronged, or something has happened that you feel is totally unfair. Maturity is being able to realize that loss is horrible, and unfair things happen everyday. A divorce happens to an innocent mate, a family member is killed, a cherished family member or friend dies unexpectedly, someone has to watch a loved one go through a painful illness, a friend or family member is assaulted, relationships falter, terrible accidents happen unexpectedly. Heartbreaking situations of loss happen in life . . . and many times it *is* totally unfair and shouldn't have happened. You cannot afford to allow a root of bitterness to grow in your heart because it will take you captive and never release you! For your sake, please understand that life is rarely fair. You cannot afford to stay in the bitterness, blame, or self-pity mode if you are to move into genuine healing. You can't take pure water (all the healing steps that you've taken) and mix it with sewer water (bitterness, lack of forgiveness, blame, self-pity, etc) then still expect it to be good water to drink. Your hard earned progress has the ability to

digress over time if you don't come to the understanding that bad things simply happen. Although painful things in life happen, it's important to realize that life is not over. God *does* have the ability to renew your hope, faith, joy, and life, as you sincerely submit to His purpose for your life. With all of the progress you have made, choose to release any bitterness, blame, or self-pity you have been holding on to. Ask God to cleanse your heart of the feelings and attitudes that are preventing you from making lasting progress. You're going to need all the clean water of maturity you can get because next up is running.

9. Running—You've looked up to God and sought out His help. You've figured out that something has got to give. You've admitted to yourself your loss and what it meant to you, you have thoroughly felt what you needed to feel, and you realized you wanted a better life. Next you came up with a list of people who you felt could help you during (and through) your grief recovery and enlisted their help. With the help of trusted family, friends, pastors, or professionals, you learned how to stand on your own two feet again and realized that with God's help you're going to eventually be okay. You now have chosen to view grief through the eyes of maturity, realizing that bad things can happen to good people, and that loss is not a respecter of anybody. Finally, you are learning how to live life once again, and you are learning how to breathe in spite of life knocking the breath out of you. You are finally at a place of truly getting your breath and your life back. There will still be times when your grief will resurface, but it will not have the bitter sting that it once had. It no longer controls you because now you are not Grief-controlled, you are God-guided. You are learning new ways everyday to grow from your grief and new ways to enjoy life. You will never forget your loved one. In fact, you are living your life in honor of them.

10. Running the Race—Philippians 3:13-14, *"Brethren, I do not count myself to have apprehended; but one thing I do, forgetting those things which are behind and reaching forward to those things which are ahead, I press toward the goal for the prize of the upward call of God in Christ Jesus."* (NKJV) Now that we have mastered the first nine baby steps, we have finally moved forward, and are at a place where we now have the ability to help others in their grief recovery.

We have a special calling on our lives and a divine purpose. Since God has shown us the way out of deep grief, we now have the precious ability of knowing how to empathize and comfort our family and friends. We understand how to offer hope to those who are hurting. We are still learning more and more from God, because we realize our great need for God . . . not only through times of grief, but through every season of our lives. We don't just need Him, we thoroughly love and enjoy Him too. Congratulations! You have reached your goal: with God's love, mercy, grace, and help, you have truly regained your breath back that life knocked out of you!

Time will continue to move forward—your decision to have the courage to move forward now will make the difference in your grief recovery for you and your loved ones. Time doesn't heal all wounds—your decision to trust God, learning and growing through your grief process, and making the decision to move forward with your grief experience is what will provide the healing you need. Don't squander, waste, or forget any lesson you have learned through your experience with grief, and don't waste any time—you have a life to begin living and enjoying once again. Make the most of every opportunity and be wise with how you choose to spend your time. God has a specific will for your life, but it is up to you to seek His heart. Take time to set some personal life goals, as God leads you, so that you have the ability and mindset to live life to the best of your ability. Seek God with your entire heart to find out what His will is, it is there you will find *true* life.

Ephesians 5:14-17, *"This is why it is said, "Wake up, sleeper, rise from the dead, and Christ will shine on you." Be very careful, then, how you live—not as unwise but as wise, making the most of every opportunity, because the days are evil. Therefore do not be foolish, but understand what the Lord's will is."* (NIV)

"Lord, sometimes I feel as though time is frozen and my grief will never have an end or true relief. Give me the grace to seek You and Your wisdom during this cold time in my life. Be with each and every decision I make. Give me Your grace to not make any major decisions until I have a right mindset, and the clear ability to make important decisions. Lord, it is so frustrating to wait for my grief to run its course, some days I just want to quit. When days of discouragement come upon

Live life to the fullest!

me, please pour Your encouragement into me, and give me Your grace to be patient. Give me the wisdom to best know how to invest my time, and give me the discernment to learn the lessons You have for me while I wait . . . Help me to be still and know that You are God. Thank You for giving me a new perspective on time, and help me to eventually have the ability to live my life to the fullest, making the most of every single day and opportunity. As I begin to live my life more purposefully and fully, may I praise You for how you have worked my grief out in Your perfect timing. In Jesus Name, Amen"

3 Oxygens

1. Take the time you need to thoroughly grieve before making any big decisions. Be patient with yourself and ask God for wisdom in the decisions you'll be making.

2. Remove the timetables for your grief and do not limit your grief. Grief has the ability to teach you valuable lessons that you simply cannot learn any other way. Embrace the lessons you learn through grief and allow God to mold your heart throughout your grief experience in His timing.

3. Take the time you need to understand your grief, to self reflect, and ask for God's help in setting life goals while taking small baby steps of progress each and every day.

CHAPTER 9

~

The Oxygen of Forgiveness

If there is to be any true long-lasting freedom and healing, it is of great importance to make the decision to live a life of forgiveness. You may need to forgive others—or you may need to forgive yourself. You may even need to seek forgiveness from others. It may be necessary to work out your relationship with God. You can make great strides in your grief recovery, *but* if you stay stuck in bitterness towards God, others, or yourself, you will eventually swing back to square one.

I have found that issues of grief and loss can be complex when also battling forgiveness issues at the same time. Choosing not to have a heart of forgiveness, while working out your grief, places you on a crazy roller coaster ride that you will not be able to stop . . . until you work out the issues of forgiveness and bitterness in your heart.

You may be upset with yourself, a family member, friend, medical professional, or another person that caused your loss to take place. You may be angry at your loved one for leaving you to live life without them—you may even be extremely angry with God and blame Him for your loss and pain. When loss occurs, we want to blame something or someone for our pain. Sometimes, the blame is properly placed—while other times, people or God may unfairly become an object of blame for our pain and heartache. It is okay to be angry or frustrated about a loved one dying, or a circumstance of loss in your life, but if you are to truly get your breath back, you will need to release any bitterness from your heart.

Releasing bitterness can be difficult at times, but consider this: when you choose to not forgive or release your bitterness, the roots of bitterness deepen everyday and eventually grow to take over your heart, spirit, mind, and even health to the point of changing who you are as a person. If you allow a person or situation to change who you are due to bitterness, you will not have the ability to experience (or carry out) God's perfect will for your life . . . and your relationship with God will be compromised. You have a specific purpose in life that *only you* can fulfill. Instead of pouring your efforts into holding on to your bitterness, pour your time and energy into God. He has the power to make all things right and new. Trust Him to open and close the doors that He wants opened and closed for you. Don't waste your time being bitter or unforgiving . . . or trying to get somebody to be sorry, or to pay for their offense. It is a dead end road that will leave *you* stuck. Give the person or situation over to God and ask Him to carry out His perfect will for your life and circumstance. Ask God to free you from bitterness. You may be wondering how on earth you are going to muster up the ability to forgive the person or the situation that altered your heart and life. In life-altering situations of loss, I personally do not think it is possible to forgive or move forward without help and grace from God. I encourage you to ask God for an extra measure of grace to forgive those that have offended or hurt you. Ask God to guide you in forgiving others and ask Him to give you the grace to move forward.

It is so important to allow God to help you to forgive others because you cannot camp out in bitterness . . . you will ultimately destroy yourself. Work out your anger by pouring your heart out to God. Plead with Him for His help, ask Him to reveal to you how to move forward, and ask Him for an extra measure of grace to forgive. If you are struggling with anger towards God, sit down and have an honest conversation with Him. He knows what you are thinking and He understands exactly where you are in your grief process. Nothing you think, say, or feel is going to surprise Him. Respectably work out your grief with God as honorably as you can.

Sometimes the hardest person to forgive is yourself. I went through agonizing guilt after my sister died because I had not been there for her when she needed me most. I had to force myself to come to terms with my poor decisions. My regrets and guilt haunted me—and it took me years before I was able to forgive myself. One day as I reflected on how badly I had let her down, the thought came to me, S*he would have forgiven me.* Why then was it so hard to forgive myself? I had to realize the truth that my sister would not have wanted me to be depressed or guilt laden. She was so full of life and enjoyed living so much. My sister would have been so disappointed in me for wasting my life in an ocean of guilt and regrets. It would be a complete slap to her face if I were to waste my life when she doesn't have the opportunity to live life on earth anymore. I know my sister would want for me (and the rest of our family) to be living life and experiencing joy. Your loved one would want the same for you, they would want for you to live the best life possible and for you to live life as fully as you can! After self reflecting and working on the issue of my guilt, I made the commitment to forgive myself and to live life in honor of her. Since she no longer has the ability to live life, then I am never going to take life for granted. I truly feel as though a deceased loved one would say, *I do not want for you to be sad or depressed, I want you to live life to the fullest. Of course, I want you to remember me and what my life meant to you, but more importantly, I want you to live life in honor of me. I want you to forgive yourself and not take life for granted—I don't want for you to waste life. I know it's hard, but please forgive yourself and keep living and enjoying life!*

We need to realize that our loved ones no longer think from an earthly perspective. *What might have upset them on earth does not upset them now.* If there was conflict on earth, they no longer hold it against us. My sister is probably shaking her head and wondering why it took me so long to forgive myself. *She would've forgiven me from day one.* Life is too short and fleeting to spend it being depressed, hateful, bitter, somber, or filled with guilt or regrets. Yes, regrets and guilt are common emotions during grief, but we need to develop an eternal mindset. I don't know your circumstances, but I can't stress enough that you need to forgive yourself if you are holding on to regrets or guilt. Work your issues of regret or guilt out, seeking pastoral care or professional counsel if need be. Forgiveness of yourself, or others, is so very important because without doing so, your progress will be limited. How do you truly get through your regrets or guilt? To overcome my regrets and guilt, I wrote down every regret I had in life. I then talked to God about each regret and sought His forgiveness, laying my guilt and regrets at His alter. I took the time to make any regrets or guilt I was carrying "right"—I asked others who were living to forgive me for times I had failed them, I then asked God to ask my loved ones in Heaven to forgive me for anything I had regretted. I asked God to tell my sister I was sorry for any way that I had failed her and I asked Him to tell her how much I love her. I then asked Him to ask my sister to forgive me. I chose to forgive myself and made the commitment to never make the same mistakes that left me with guilt and regret in the first place. The most important thing I asked of God was this: I asked Him to forgive me for my negligence in taking my loved ones for granted and I purposed to change. At times I'm sure my family tires of me telling them I love them, or hugging them so often, but I truly learned a difficult life lesson. It was a very freeing feeling to choose to make positive changes in response to my new commitment and it really allowed me to significantly heal once I allowed myself to let go of the guilt and regrets I had built up.

If you are struggling through guilt or regrets and are wondering if there was anything you could have done differently to keep a loved one from dying, let me assure you that there is nothing you could have done to prevent their death. Psalm 139:16 says, *"You saw me before I was born. Every day of my life was recorded in your book. Every moment was laid out before a single day had passed."* (NLT) Ecclesiastes 6:10 says, *"Everything has already been decided. It was known long ago what each person would be. So there's no use arguing with God about your destiny."* (NLT) Before a person is even born, God records every single day of their life in His book. Every moment is laid out *before* they are even born. God knows when every person is going to be born and He knows the *exact* day and time they are going to die. He knew precisely what their purpose was going to be *and* what each person was going to be . . . *He knew all of this before they even took their first breath.* Our times of birth and death are prewritten, it's part of God's greater purpose and sovereign plan. It is difficult to completely understand or comprehend God's plans or purposes, sometimes even frustrating. Although heartbreaking for those left behind, a loved one's life or death may have been used for a greater plan or purpose that might not be revealed until we get to Heaven. God's plan and purpose for each life may be confusing to us, but *it is unmistakeable to Him.*

Sometimes, life is not fair and the pain we go through is hard to come to terms with. When I began to sort through my feelings of a particular circumstance that had happened to me, I struggled with forgiveness. I did not want to extend forgiveness because what had happened hurt me terribly and forever changed my life. I wanted to grow bitter towards the person that caused me extreme personal pain—but I began to realize that this only compounded my grief and left *me* feeling exhausted, miserable, depressed, angry, and weak. For *my* personal wellbeing, it became necessary to make the decision to forgive *them*. In time, forgiving this person brought healing to my heart. I no longer had to carry the heavy burdens of bitterness. I was freed up to trust God to handle the situation as I unconditionally turned it all over to Him.

Forgiveness is rarely easy. It makes us feel as though we're letting whoever hurt or offended us off the hook—but what we're actually doing is taking them off our hook—*and putting them onto God's hook*. He has the power to deal with hurtful or offensive people. He is the ultimate judge, with the ultimate wisdom and discernment, to do what is best. God has the power to move in the hearts of those who have wronged us, or the situation that is causing us distress, as we truly give a situation or person over to Him. Completely trusting God to work through His timing and His ways, He will be faithful to work His ultimate purpose out for the pain or situation we are experiencing. When we hang onto our bitterness, we fail to allow God total freedom to work out His purposes for our situation. God gives us an important choice when it comes to difficult people or circumstances: do we want His hands in the situation to work it out . . . or ours. As long as we choose to take matters into our own hands, keeping our hands in the situation, He'll allow us to do just that, but we will become *and stay* stuck. He desires to show *His* power—not ours. Please realize that nobody gets away with anything. God will hold each person accountable for their actions, therefore we can trust Him in obeying His command to forgive others. I'm not saying it's easy to forgive others—because sometimes it isn't. Forgiveness can be one of the hardest things you will ever have to work through. The greater the hurt or offense, the more difficult it is to forgive. Forgiveness is vital—*it opens up your ability to truly work through stagnated grief.*

Sometimes, forgiveness brings relief and restores peace. Other times, it honestly is like a stinging slap to your face by a wet hand that is drenched in reality and truth—especially when the person you're forgiving isn't even sorry for their offense. Forgiveness makes you think about the total facts of what happened, realizing the worst, yet hoping for the best. Yes, it can be very hard to forgive those that have deeply wronged or hurt you—*but no one is worth destroying your peace or relationship with God, so choose to forgive them.*

My sister's first fiancé that passed away had been a successful football player. While in college, he made a seemingly small decision that would permanently consequence him for the rest of his short lived life. He made the decision to dive into a hotel swimming pool, not realizing the hotel's water level was incompetent. This decision left him a quadriplegic, meaning he became paralyzed from the neck down. Becoming paralyzed destroyed his physical life, but he said being in his wheelchair saved his spiritual life. There were many talks I had with him where his heart was filled with regret from what had happened. He shared with me how hard it was to go from being strong and able-bodied to not having the ability to do anything on his own. However, he lived a life that was free from bitterness. I asked him what made the difference between being bitter versus the peace he radiated—he shared that he trusted God's plan for his life. He said if it had not been for the diving accident, he wouldn't have as close of a relationship with God. He always hoped that some new medical discovery would make a way for him to walk again, but he chose to make the best of his situation. He would always tell my sister, *"We're not going to focus on what we can't do, we're going to focus on what we can."* Had he given up, quit, grown bitter towards God or the hotel, or felt sorry for himself, many lives never would have been changed by his amazing testimony. He held a weekly Bible study at his house where hearts were challenged every week to live fully for God. I had been attending his Bible study, not yet a Christian, but through the encouragement I received from him, my sister, my brother, and others that attended his Bible study, I was able to see a remarkable difference in their lives. I'm not sure I would have gotten saved had it not been for my amazing family, my sister's fiancé, and my friends from his Bible study. Their testimonies made a great impact in my life. There is something powerful about a testimony where a hardship takes place in a life, and they choose to forgive and draw close to God. You can see God in their hearts and the way they live. They shine so very brightly and people are drawn to that. That's what drew me to this Bible study—I saw a difference in my sister, my brother, and my sister's fiancé. Through my sister's fiancé's obedience to God to tell others his testimony—lives were changed, hearts were saved, and people were encouraged to love God. Many that came to the Bible study are now in full time ministry and one is being greatly used by God as a lead vocalist with the praise band Passion. All were beautifully influenced from one man's testimony of forgiveness—and his willingness to serve God *through his hardship.* After hosting his weekly Bible study for a few years, my sister's fiancé was in a car accident and died after a year of being in the hospital. His testimony is still a bright light to those that knew him, you never forget a testimony like his.

I know it's hard to forgive others, and as I already said, even harder to forgive yourself. I've never met one person yet who thinks, *"Today I get the pure joy of realizing how terrible my life has become due to my own choices"* or *"Someone's negligence or selfishness has forever changed my life and I get the joy of dealing with loss!"* Life is very difficult at times and is sometimes difficult to forgive. Life is hard when the only thing you can think is, *"How am I ever going to want to get out of bed? I can't stand living when I know my entire day is one big remembrance of my loss."* Each situation of loss is horribly painful—but you will find that forgiveness is vital if you are ever going to have the ability to live life fully once again. It simply isn't fair to carry around a heavy yoke of bitterness that further damages every intricate part of your heart and life. Sometimes people choose not to forgive because they believe that forgiving means forgetting or accepting what happened. Forgiveness is not forgetting or accepting someone's hurtful or damaging behavior. It is releasing the person or situation unconditionally into God's hands. Sometimes people choose not to forgive themselves because they believe they are making an atonement for what they feel regretful or guilty about. *That is not how God or your loved one would want you to live.* After my sister died, I truly believed that the worse I could feel about letting her down, the more sorry I could be. Punishing yourself for the rest of your life will not reverse what happened in your past. In fact, *punishing yourself prevents others from hearing the testimony that God has planned for you.* God has the power to turn your greatest regrets and guilt into a powerful message that will help, encourage, and inspire others. If we trust God when we're at rock bottom in the valleys of guilt and regrets, *God gets the unmistakable glory for lifting us up.* Ask Him to raise you up from the pits of bitterness, depression, guilt, regret, and discouragement.

Some of you may be very angry with yourselves or God. It is so important to work out your relationship with God and yourself. I know I emphasize this a lot but it is so important that you grasp what I am saying: Pour your heart out to God, do whatever it takes to make your relationship with Him right. He already knows how you feel and He knows your every thought—make peace with God. He gets a lot of blame for situations that are not His fault. For example, I have a friend whose spouse committed adultery and divorced her. My friend was so angry at God for allowing her husband to devastate her. God loves each of us so much that He allows each of us the gift of free will—no one is a robot or a puppet. God did not hurt my friend, *her spouse did.* I truly believe that God sometimes allows a heartache or tragedy to occur in our lives to prevent a greater heartache or tragedy from happening in the future. I sincerely believe that some of the losses we go through in life are unseen acts of mercy on God's part . . . or divine protection from future circumstances of hurt. We will finally have the ability to see the entire bigger picture once we enter God's presence.

It is easy to feel as though God has betrayed or abandoned you, but let me assure you that nothing is further from the truth. I went through times of struggling with intense anger towards God. I blamed Him for allowing painful circumstances in my life that I felt were totally unfair. It was hard while growing up to go through various trials and losses that left me hurt, confused, and frustrated. I felt as though God cared very little about me, as though He was very far away. I felt that I was unimportant, like I didn't have any significant value to Him. I was angry at God when He called those that I love home to Heaven. I wasn't ready for them to die. I wish I could still talk to my sister on the phone, I seriously miss her. I wish I could have had more time with her, my dad, and other loved ones. Losing someone you love is heartbreaking and may threaten to leave you a bitter depressed mess. I slowly became bitter towards God and initially resented each and every loss I went through—until I understood and accepted the truth that God has a much bigger and higher plan than I can wrap my limited mind around. In times of heartache, it can feel as though God is not being faithful in keeping His promises, but we need to consider two truths: God always keeps His promises and God may have higher plans where a promise may not be fulfilled until Heaven.

God's ways are not our ways and His thoughts are not our thoughts. His purposes are wiser and so much higher than we can ever comprehend. Isaiah 55:8-13 explains it best, *"For my thoughts are not your thoughts, neither are your ways my ways," declares the LORD. "As the heavens are higher than the earth, so are my ways higher than your ways and my thoughts than your thoughts. As the rain and the snow come down from heaven, and do not return to it without watering the earth and making it bud and flourish, so that it yields seed for the sower and bread for the eater, so is my word that goes out from my mouth: It will not return to me empty, but will accomplish what I desire and achieve the purpose for which I sent it. You will go out in joy and be led forth in peace; the mountains and hills will burst into song before you, and all the trees of the field will clap their hands. Instead of the thornbush will grow the juniper, and instead of briers the myrtle will grow. This will be for the LORD's renown, for an everlasting sign, that will endure forever."* (NIV)

I love the last part of this passage of scripture that states . . . *"Instead of the thornbush will grow the juniper, and instead of briers the myrtle will grow. This will be for the LORD's renown, for an everlasting sign, that will endure forever."* God *will* take away the thorny pain of grief and replace it with beauty as we submit to Him for His renown which will endure forever.

I'm not suggesting that anybody ever completely overcomes their grief because grief is like a scar. It will always be a part of you. *True grief recovery, in my opinion, is learning how to heal, forgive, live, and love life, with God's help, in spite of the heartaches and trials that one goes through.* It is having the ability to see the good that is remaining in life and being grateful for it. It is experiencing life and seeing the beauty in even the smallest things. Step by step, encouragement by encouragement, you can overcome bitterness, and other negative emotions that grief throws your way, so you will finally be free to fully experience life again.

You don't have to continue to struggle through your grief. Allow God to heal the pain, guilt, and regrets you are facing due to your grief and circumstances. Seek Him with everything in you—pray to Him, read His Word, gain as much wisdom and understanding as you possibly can through His Word, obey Him, love and praise Him, thank Him for anything good in your life—this truly is your starting point to genuine healing. Pour your heart out to God, asking Him to give you the grace to live a life of forgiveness, and allow Him to work out your grief. It may be painful, humbling, confusing, relieving, comforting, or any other assortment of emotions. Be prepared to go through a myriad of feelings when working out all issues of life, grief, and forgiveness with God. God truly is in every detail of your life and you can trust Him with every detail of your grief recovery. He is your true hope of obtaining the *lasting* oxygen you need to getting your breath back from grief and the trials you face in life.

Ask God right now to help you pick up the pieces of your shattered life. He is more than willing and able to help you through any and every situation of loss. All you have to do is seek Him with your whole heart and ask. He has deep, rich truths to share with you—but first you have to clean your heart of any bitterness so that His Word and love can sink in. Think of your heart as a sponge . . . if you have bitterness in your heart, that is what your heart has absorbed . . . whatever is in your heart *will lead your life*. "Wring" the bitterness out of your heart and ask God to fill it up with His love, mercy, and the fruits of His Spirit . . . *absorb Him.* It is shortly after that you will have a new measure of grace and ability to forgive others.

The more tragic the loss, the more time will be needed to heal and forgive. If a person is in a car accident . . . say a fender bender . . . they may need a few stitches, *but* if a person is in a head on collision at full speed, they may need to be hospitalized for months, require numerous surgeries, possibly even physical rehabilitation. Forgiveness is a lot like this analogy. Some offenses in life are small and require very little to forgive another person. Other offenses radically alter the course of your life and it will take God providing an extra measure of grace to forgive the offense. God may need to do "surgery" on your heart and "rehabilitate" your mind. He may need to help you transition from a worldly ability to forgive over to an eternal perspective of forgiveness. When my sister died, it was not difficult to forgive her doctors because I realized they were seriously trying to save her life. When people have knowingly done something to hurt me . . . knowing the result would cause me great pain . . . that has been much more difficult to forgive.

forgiveness is life . .

If we're honest with ourselves, sometimes it takes a lot to forgive others. We need Someone greater to lead us on the paths of forgiveness. It is through His grace in our lives we will find the strength to forgive. If we are to truly have the ability to forgive, it is so important to realize that challenges and trials in life do not "just happen" . . . and they are not meant to confuse, harm, or destroy you. They are God-entrusted lessons to build your character, so that through these lessons you will have the strengthened ability to know God fuller, to accomplish God's ultimate purpose and will for your life. It is very common to struggle through accepting God's will in times of grief, but please allow me to encourage you to embrace it. I once heard at a seminar a great definition of God's Perfect Will: *God's perfect will for your life is exactly what you would want if you knew all the facts.* As we seek to forgive, we need to remember that everything we have been allowed to go through has a divine purpose—*and God knows all of the facts.*

God can teach you lessons during times of loss that you could never hope to learn any other way. There truly are benefits during times of grief. When someone has died or has hurt you, it is an opportunity to refine and prioritize your life. I have learned many rich valuable lessons as a result of grief. I have learned to put my trust in God instead of people—people will fail, God will not. I learned to never blindly trust others—and how to use discernment. Going through my son's medical crises as well as my own health issues—I have learned the importance of health and wellness and to never take life or a loved one for granted. Not having my dad as a child and having regrets from my sister's last days—I learned how to put family first . . . if any of my family needs me, I'm there. I learned the hard way to put people first and to make my loved ones a top priority. Due to being devastated by the actions of others, I learned the priceless lessons of wisdom, mercy, and forgiveness. *For every bad situation that happens, there is a life lesson to be learned.* It is through grief, loss, and forgiveness that you will learn some of life's greatest lessons—if you are willing to learn from God and trust Him in forgiving others.

When your grief overwhelms you and you feel utterly hopeless, remember James 4:14, *"Yet you do not know what your life will be like tomorrow. You are just a vapor that appears for a little while and then vanishes away."* (NASB) Life on earth is extremely short and fleeting compared to eternity. To illustrate this point, take the palm of your hand and hold it up to your mouth. Now let out a short breath onto your palm. That is all our earthly lives are when compared to eternity. Life is a mere vapor, a mist. The horrendous heartache you are feeling right now will not last forever. The regret, guilt, and bitterness you may feel in your heart today does not have to plague you forever. You can't go back and change the past—*but you can learn from it—and by doing so change your future.* The important thing is to not waste your life reveling in bitterness or depression. *Change what needs to be changed, do things different.* If there is someone you need to forgive, forgive them. Love when you have the opportunity to love. Live when you have the opportunity to live. If you can't learn to live with yourself, or find the strength to live for others, then please live in honor of the one you lost. If something or someone has knocked all the living breath out of you, don't tolerate it any longer—get your breath back! Acknowledge your loss, deal with it head on. If there is something you can do to make the situation better, then do whatever you can. If you can't do anything to make it better, accept it or give it to God. Feel what you need to feel. If you have trusted family and friends to help you though your grief, invite them to go through your grief experience alongside you. Do what you can with the resources you have available. Work through your hurt, frustration, bitterness, and feelings, continually taking an inventory of your life. One of the greatest benefits of grief and loss is you realize who and what is truly important in life. Grief clarifies everything about life, relationships, and priorities. *Loss truly puts life in perspective.* Forgiveness further clarifies life.

Some of the most healing byproducts of forgiveness are: feeling the freedom and lightness of soul that accompanies your decision to forgive, a closer relationship to God, a lighter disposition, strengthened character, a softened heart, and a peaceful spirit. Please don't waste one more day of your life being unforgiving. You're not punishing God, the situation, or the person that hurt or offended you—*you're hurting, punishing, and imprisoning yourself.* You are not promised tomorrow so please don't waste another day: forgive others, forgive yourself, make peace with God.

Hebrews 4:16, *"Let us then approach the throne of grace with confidence, so that we may receive mercy and find grace to help us in our time of need."* (NIV) God will help you to find the grace and help you need to accomplish truly forgiving others. Seek God with your whole heart and ask Him to give you the strength and grace to work out the emotions that are harming you. Ask Him to give you the wisdom to know the best way of *fully* forgiving the people and situations you are going through. Realize that forgiveness is sometimes a process. After making the initial decision to forgive (act of your will), you then may have to work through the feelings of that decision (act of your heart). Work your feelings out with God by your side, doing what you need to do to *align* your *will* and your *heart.*

With all grief and loss, you have two choices: you can live to feed your grief and bitterness *or* you can choose to feed life and truly live. This doesn't mean that as soon as you forgive others, or yourself, you will instantly be over your grief and loss—it means you realize you cannot ever go back and make whatever happened not happen, and that you are choosing to get your quality of life back. How does one go about aligning their will with their heart? When times of discouragement or bitterness try to set in, choose to say, *"I choose to forgive others. I am going to learn from each and every grief and loss experience and grow from it. Yes, horrible things have happened. Yes, I have gone through the deaths of my loved ones—and sometimes life has not been fair—but if I keep beating myself up, or not forgiving others, then all of these situations have defeated me and killed my hope! It's bad enough these things have happened, but I WILL get my breath back so that I can breathe and fully live life! Therefore, I choose to forgive others and I choose to forgive myself so that I don't waste precious time. I choose forgiveness because God has forgiven me, I choose love, and ultimately, I choose LIFE!"* We have the ability to make a strong declaration like that when we make God first place in our lives.

Ephesians 5:15-20 is an amazing section of scripture that offers excellent instruction: *"Be very careful, then, how you live—not as unwise but as wise, making the most of every opportunity, because the days are evil. Therefore do not be foolish, but understand what the Lord's will is. Do not get drunk on wine, which leads to debauchery. Instead, be filled with the Spirit, speaking to one another with psalms, hymns, and songs from the Spirit. Sing and make music from your heart to the Lord, always giving thanks to God the Father for everything, in the name of our*

Lord Jesus Christ." (NIV) I have been amazed at how many sections of scripture are useful for grief recovery, as well as issues of guilt, regrets, and forgiveness. Ephesians 5:15-20 tells us to be very careful in how we live. We can view this as another blueprint for grief recovery as we personalize this section of scripture for times of loss: be careful for how you live, live life to the fullest because the days are evil, don't waste your grief or any lesson you can learn through grief, make the most of a grief experience. Seek to understand what God's will is for what you go through in life. Don't waste your life on getting drunk, or other substances to help you through the pain of your grief . . . instead, take the opportunity to live life to forgive and encourage others, delighting in the Lord, and thanking God for everything.

If you continually struggle with forgiveness and bitterness issues, you will find that seeking wise counsel from a Christian therapist or respected pastor can be very helpful. Sometimes, we need additional help when we are not able to work out issues on our own. Seeking pastoral care and professional help simultaneously is often helpful and beneficial. There are times when you may not have the ability to understand a solution from one person, but you may be able to from another source of help. God made each of us to have the ability to relate to different people at different levels. Find the additional sources of help you need and never quit. You deserve to have a life of peace that you enjoy living. God truly wants that for you, it is His desire that you live and experience an abundant life, regardless of whatever heartbreaking situation you are going through. John 10:10 says, *"The thief's purpose is to steal and kill and destroy. My purpose is to give them a rich and satisfying life."* (NLT) It is God's plan for you to have life in all its fullness. Seek God and the resources you need to get your breath back. Life may have knocked your breath out of you, but with God's help, and the resources He graciously makes available to you, you have the ability to get your breath and life back. Do not waste another day of your life, for your life is way too valuable to waste.

"Heavenly Father, I know that I have hurt You so many times over the course of my life. I'm sincerely sorry and ask You to fully forgive me. I also ask for, and thank you for, your mercy and grace along with Your forgiveness. Please help me to fully forgive those that have hurt or offended me. Lord, sometimes it feels impossible to forgive those that

have forever altered my life, but I realize I need to forgive them this very moment and release them to You . . . I choose right now to take them off of my hook and place them onto Your hook. I'm removing my hands from the situation and placing the situation unconditionally into Your hands. If I have harbored bitterness in my soul, I ask You to forgive me right now, and I plead with You to cleanse me of all bitterness, guilt, regrets, and resentments. I choose to trust You and I choose to forgive all others right now. Help me to realize and remember that people are fallible and that I am fallible too. Help me to also realize that nothing in my life is merely circumstance, for you have a divine purpose as stated in Ecclesiastes 6:10, "Everything has already been decided. It was known long ago what each person would be. So there's no use arguing with God about your destiny." (NLT) Give me an extra measure of Your grace to never argue about Your will for my life . . . help me to trust Your plan for the entirety of my life. Heal my heart, Lord, make me new. Begin a new work in my life and light my path with mercy, forgiveness, and grace. Help me to extend forgiveness, mercy, and grace to others. Thank You for being my truest, most loyal Friend. Continually bring Your fresh healing into my heart and life. Reward me as I transition into forgiving others and seeking You. Your Word says that the days are evil and to make the most of every opportunity. Lord, help me to accomplish this. Grant me Your strength. Sometimes in my grief, I am so worn out, frustrated, and distracted. Give me Your grace to begin living life to the fullest once again, making the most of every opportunity. With Your love and help, I can do this! I love You, Lord. In Jesus Name, Amen." (NLT)

3 Oxygens

1. Take time with God to truly sort through any struggles you are having with forgiveness and bitterness. Whether you are struggling with forgiving yourself, family members, others, a situation, or life challenge . . . or struggling with bitterness towards God, work it out with God and ask Him to grant you the grace you need to forgive . . . asking Him to remove all bitterness from your heart. If you are still struggling with bitterness or depression after seeking God and forgiving, seek pastoral care, wise counsel, or the professional help and resources you need to truly resolve your bitterness so you can truly live life.

2. Every loss and life challenge is an opportunity to learn new life lessons. What life lessons can you learn through your situation and what commitments of change can you make? Make positive changes in response to your new commitment.

3. God has the power to turn your grief into a powerful message that will help, encourage, and inspire others. Ask God to develop a testimony in your heart for His Renown.

CHAPTER 10

~

The Oxygen of Enjoying Life Through Traditions & Wellness

I purposely saved this chapter for last because most people do not want to hear about traditions, wellness, or enjoyment while going through intense grief. Those in the fiery furnace of grief know firsthand that grief is not enjoyable and many doubt if they will ever feel well again—much less have the ability to truly enjoy life . . . *or anything* . . . again. I will tell you that as time goes by, you *will* be able to truly enjoy life once again. You probably don't think that's true right now in the midst of your grief, *but in time,* you will have the ability to fully live, love, and enjoy life. I remember after two major losses thinking that I would never be able to fully enjoy life again. After one of these losses, someone told me that I would feel better in time, and that the pain from this particular loss wouldn't plague or consume my day the way it was at the time. I didn't feel as though I had the ability to enjoy life—*in fact, I felt as though I was dead but couldn't die.* Even though I was going through intense grief, I knew I still had the ability to be grateful, so I made a decision to find five things at the end of each day that I was truly grateful to God for. I *needed* to find my ability to be grateful for the gift of life again. I began to see how precious life truly is—and after a period of time, I realized that I was once again finding enjoyment in everyday life. I began to be more and more grateful for the good in my life, especially my loved ones who helped me through that intensely sad time. Gratefulness played a big part in the amount of times I thought about my pain. I went from thinking about this particular loss hundreds of times a day to just a couple of times a day. Gratefulness through this particular loss put perspective in my life, almost as though I had put on a set of glasses that made life crystal clear. I found out that grief and loss were not designed to frustrate, harm, or discourage me—they were actually powerful motivators to live my life as fully and purposefully as I could. Gratefulness truly puts life in crystal clear perspective and motivates you to live life wisely.

There are many valuable lessons you can learn through your heartaches and trials, as well as many treasures gleaned. *Lessons and treasures learned through grief are gifts in disguise that teach you to live a fuller and more purposeful life.* The deeper you dig into God's Word and heart, the more hidden treasure is to be found. For every grief experience you go through, you gain more insight of how to live and achieve a better life. The ultimate lesson and treasure gained through grief is learning how to better love, understand, and enjoy God. Growing through grief, one fully understands that tomorrow is never guaranteed so today is a once in a lifetime opportunity—a gift from God to be lived to the fullest.

Many who have gone through grief have a hard time enjoying life, especially if their loss left them with unsettled feelings. Loss is such a hard thing to go through. It threatens to leave you isolated, stuck in your grief, unable to relate to others, and unable to enjoy life—but it is not fair to yourself or those around you to give up or quit on life. Work out all unsettled feelings to the best of your ability, forgive others and yourself, and be patient with yourself and others. *Life is worth living, and is even worth celebrating, regardless of loss. Just having the gift of life is reason enough to live and celebrate.* You may feel as though you shouldn't feel better or that it is even wrong to feel better. You may even feel as though you do not deserve to enjoy life since your loved one died. You may feel guilty with every smile, joy, or happiness that you experience, but please make the decision today to learn how to live life again. Understand that it truly is okay to allow yourself to live life fully after going through loss. Be kind to yourself, take steps forward—even if they are baby steps, and stop punishing yourself. All of the sadness, tears, self-sacrificing, self-punishment, and depression in the world cannot bring your loved one back or erase your loss. It is so hard to let the past go and move forward, at times it is even uncomfortable or scary, but you deserve to have joy and wellness in your life. You are valuable and your life is precious. You have a life purpose that only you can fulfill—if you remain stuck in your grief, nobody else has the capability of fulfilling your purpose for you . . . *you are the only one that has the ability to accomplish your life purpose.* God still has a plan for your life, but He desires for you to be actively involved in that plan.

It's easy to falsely believe that the length of time we grieve a loved one's death *is equal to* the amount and extent that we loved them. Grieving for extended long periods of time does not prove the depth of our love or loyalty to our loved one—living life in their honor is what our loved ones would have wanted for us instead. Living life in a loved one's honor does *not* mean that we forget about our loved one. Living life in their honor means that we want to celebrate their life, memory, and the many ways they were a special part of our lives. By doing activities we once enjoyed with them, we are able to connect to the memories that are now treasured in our hearts. Living life to the fullest prevents wasting our lives and brings honor to God, our deceased loved ones, and the lives God is still blessing us with.

Loss, and learning how to get your breath back, is very hard at first—but after you make small decisions, little by little, to live and celebrate life in spite of your grief and circumstances, you find that life eventually becomes easier to truly live. In time, life can take on a new meaning.

Grief genuinely changes all who have deeply experienced it—you may find that you think and feel differently than before you had experienced deep loss. As a result of my grief, my thoughts about God, goals, interests, time, plans, purpose, relationships, and life have all changed—and I have found that my loss and grief have developed a depth in my perspective. Something else I have found, as a result of my grief, is that I have a much larger capacity to appreciate life, much more than had I never experienced grief or loss. When we properly respond to grief and loss, our life takes on a new and deeper meaning as we are keenly more aware of God's purpose for our grief and life—*those who walk through grief with God are no longer content with allowing relationships, opportunities, lessons, or life to be wasted.* Life takes on a whole new meaning and the desire to want to live life in a new fullness transpires.

As we begin to desire to live life fully for God's purpose, and in honor of our loved ones, we realize the need for wellness. Something that took me by surprise during my grief is that due to depression, I lost most forms of wellness in my life. The more I became totally lost in my grief, the more I lost my optimal health. It is very common after a death to neglect our health. Being preoccupied with grief counters any wellness concerns. Unfortunately, wellness is not a top priority when your heart is breaking . . . *but it should be.* It is very important to take care of yourself during times of grief, depression, and stress by incorporating wellness, exercise, and good nutrition into your daily life (talk to your doctor before you begin any exercise or nutrition plan and ask your doctor what exercises are best for you). If you are to live life to the fullest, and accomplish God's best for your life, wellness will need to be implemented and honored.

Some of you may be new to understanding what wellness is. Wellness is spiritual, physical, emotional, and mental wellbeing—living life well. God, family, friends, health, nutrition, exercise, enjoyment, traditions, grief recovery, relaxation, and a wise schedule are all facets of living life well—these are all components of wellness . . . and all will help you to get your breath back after life knocks it out of you. I like to describe wellness as ridding your life of all toxicity (toxic thoughts and decisions, toxic foods, toxic schedules, toxic living, toxic addictions, etc) and replacing all toxicity with edification. Edification is allowing good people and good things into your life to build you up, and to establish, strengthen, and uplift your life. If there are toxic or destructive decisions, food, lifestyle, unwise schedules, addictions, or any other negative toxins in your life, it is time to pray about how best to deal with these issues. For optimal wellness, you will need to take full responsibility for your life and dedicate your life to God. Philippians 4:8-9 is a good starting indicator of how to live a life of wellness, *"Summing it all up, friends, I'd say you'll do best by filling your minds and meditating on things true, noble, reputable, authentic, compelling, gracious—the best, not the worst; the beautiful, not the ugly; things to praise, not things to curse. Put into practice what you learned from me, what you heard and saw and realized. Do that, and God, who makes everything work together, will work you into his most excellent harmonies."* (MSG) Fill your minds with things that are good and praiseworthy: *all things that are true, noble, right, pure, lovely, and honorable.* This passage of scripture is useful when deciding what type of thoughts, feelings, or activities we allow into our lives when setting the boundaries of wellness.

(handwritten margin notes:) WELLNESS! / Focus your thoughts on things worthy of Praise! / Fruit of the Spirit

I cannot stress how important wellness is during times of grief. In times of grief, a person is more susceptible to depression and becoming ill. Be sure to take the time to ensure your wellness. Proper nutrition and exercise works wonders for how a person feels physically, mentally, and emotionally, and can improve your mood, while restoring or maintaining your health. You can incorporate wellness by spending time with God, family, and friends, taking good care of yourself, eating right, practicing proper hygiene, exercising, getting enough sleep, doing enjoyable activities, maintaining a wise schedule, and relaxing Wellness is simply feeling well, living well, and enjoying life. There are many ways that you can begin to incorporate wellness. God, life, marriage, parenting, family, church, friends, hobbies, community, and health are all gifts that were designed to be enjoyed to the fullest. What can you do to enjoy and delight in these gifts today? Spending time talking to God, reading His Word, enjoying His creation, and praising Him are ways to enjoy Him. If you are blessed with family, marriage, children, friends, or community, take time today to enrich these relationships. Plan an outing with a loved one, taking the time to enjoy your relationship. Think of ways to delight in building your church up, see what needs they have, then fulfill those needs through service or contributions. Minister to fellow church members through encouragement and hospitality. Think of your hobbies and interests that you enjoyed before your loss. Take the time to enjoy your hobbies and interests once again—you may even want to take up a new hobby. If you are married, have children, or extended family, involve them and ask if they'd like to join you in your activities. They may not be ready to participate or they may appreciate the opportunity to join you in incorporating wellness. If you can create a new way of life, and incorporate wellness, with your spouse, children, and family, you will find that there is healing in bonding while enjoying activities with your family. Learn new ways to have fun with your family and create new experiences and opportunities to enjoy together. One of my favorite wellness activities is walking with my family. My family and I have had some great conversations while going on walks. If you have a close friend or family member, exercising with another person keeps you accountable to take care of yourself and leads the way for some great conversations and memories. When my family (or friends) and I walk together, we talk about everything and every subject. If one of us is frustrated, we are always there to listen and brighten each other's day through encouragement and humor. If we need to vent, we patiently listen to one another and then give much needed advice. Majority of the time, we simply enjoy our walk by talking about everyday life, God, future plans, or our wellness goals for the future.

God desires for us to incorporate wellness into our lives and He *wants* us to enjoy life. God the Father is the ultimate parent! Parents delight in seeing their children enjoy life. As parents, we love to see good things happen for our children, and we enjoy giving special gifts to enrich their lives. Parents love seeing their children experience joy. *Why wouldn't God want the same for His children?* He does! He desires for each of us to experience life to the fullest! He desires that we serve to the fullest, making the most of every opportunity and situation that He entrusts to us . . . yes, even grief. Matthew 7:11 allows us a glimpse into God's heart and tells how He desires good for His children's lives, *"So if you sinful people know how to give good gifts to your children, how much more will your heavenly Father give good gifts to those who ask him."* (NLT) God ultimately desires that we love and experience Him to the fullest. The best gift we can ever be given is the amazing privilege of having a deep, special, extraordinary relationship with God! To truly experience His love through wellness is exquisite and life changing.

You will find that as you incorporate wellness, it will branch out to every facet of your life. Once you delight in God, begin to exercise, eat right, take the time to properly rest and relax, and have fun with family and friends once again, you are likely to see a difference in every area of your life.

There are many resources on wellness, so do a study on wellness and see what interests you. Many churches and fitness centers offer wellness and nutrition classes. I wholeheartedly encourage you to take responsibility for your health, find out as much as you can about fitness and nutrition, and allow God to heal your body through good health. Some who are reading this book are not able to exercise due to paralysis, illness, or disability. Do what you are able to do. You may not have the ability to apply wellness physically, but you can apply principles of sound nutrition while pursuing spiritual and emotional wellness. Reading your Bible (or listening to audio tapes or CDs of the Bible) and drawing close to God is more powerful than any other type of wellness. 1 Timothy 4:8 says, *"For physical training is of some value, but godliness has value for all things, holding promise for both the present life and the life to come."* (NIV) The ultimate in wellness is when we draw close to God, and allow Him to mold us spiritually in His image, teaching us to love Him and His ways.

Developing traditions and wellness in our lives while going through grief and loss will not only sustain you, it will revive and renew you. God desires to bless each believer with wellness during times of loss, and there are abundant opportunities to learn how to build wellness into everyday life. There is no greater opportunity to develop wellness than during times of grief, life challenges, and loss.

The Bible is filled with blueprints for how we should live, how to have harmony and peace, and how to get through any trial life throws at us. Usually when a trial knocks the breath out of us, we are ill equipped to know how to handle the situation . . . or even how to respond. When faced with a trial, there is such an overwhelming temptation to fall into depression, despair, frustration, anxiety, or bitterness. It is vital to embrace God (and your grief) so that you will have the ability to develop wellness into your grief process and life. When we make God our top priority, He guides us in our wellness efforts. Wellness has not only helped me during times of grief—but also throughout my life so I was better equipped in the future for ongoing stress and trials.

While processing and going through grief, loss, or a life challenge, it's important to remember that we have an exclusive opportunity to bring glory to God through what pains us. As we trust Him, we understand that our grief experience may not be for the ultimate good here on earth—it may be for the ultimate eternal good instead. God's Word is the ultimate wellness manual to prepare us for the ultimate wellness experience—Heaven. God's ultimate goal is for eternity and He knows exactly what it will take for as many lives to be changed for eternity. God may be using your situation of loss to draw others to Him because of your excellent witness and testimony that He entrusted to you. People may be seeing hope for the first time due to how you are trusting God through your trial. They may be seeing a genuine joy and hope in you that will draw them to the heart of God. This may give you an opportunity to share the Reason for your hope so that you are able to share Christ with them. Consider John 15:5-8, *"I am the vine; you are*

we needed Hope & God can use us for His Glory

the branches. If you remain in me and I in you, you will bear much fruit; apart from me you can do nothing. If you do not remain in me, you are like a branch that is thrown away and withers; such branches are picked up, thrown into the fire and burned. If you remain in me and my words remain in you, ask whatever you wish, and it will be done for you. This is to my Father's glory, that you bear much fruit, showing yourselves to be my disciples." (NIV) Our pain can truly be for God's gain. Our pain is not meant to frustrate, confuse, or harm us, but is often allowed so that we can gain a much larger vision and purpose for our lives so we then are able to share the gospel and show ourselves to be true disciples.

You never know how God will use a loss you have experienced for your ultimate wellness or the wellness of others. I have seen God move through family and friends as they have gone through an illness. As they frequented a hospital, they were able to share Christ with the medical professionals that cared for them or other families who also had loved ones at the hospital. I've seen family and friends who have lost their jobs and had to find new employment . . . and through their situation they met new friends who they could share Christ with. Anytime God allows a loss, it is always for a deeper reason and opportunity than we can understand or begin to comprehend. God desires for every person to come to salvation and He will sometimes allow tragedy to occur so that others can find their way to Him. I have learned through deep heartache that everything God allows, He is trustworthy. God is faithful to see us through our grief to completion. As we trust Him, He allows His purposes to unfold. God cares about every facet of your grief and desires for you to trust and obey Him through every situation. As you allow God to have total access to your heart, and become a branch that depends on the Vine, wellness begins to take root and in time will fully bloom. God is faithful to carry you through your grief and He is faithful to complete your life, from the beginning to the end. He is dedicated to developing wellness in your life . . . and a testimony. Philippians 1:6, *"being confident of this, that he who began a good work in you will carry it on to completion until the day of Christ Jesus."* (NIV)

God carrying out His perfect will for your life is something you can count on as you go through times of trials or loss. He desires for you to personally experience ultimate wellness: spiritually, mentally, physically, and emotionally. Pursuing wellness during times of grief and loss, you find out so much about yourself: your spiritual and physical condition, as well as your thoughts, beliefs, struggles, and feelings. All of these things can deceive you while going through times of grief. How do you know if your decisions are wise? How do you get to a point that you are able to think with clarity? Ask the Holy Spirit to guide you step-by-step through your thoughts, beliefs, struggles, and feelings by incorporating the fruits of the Spirit into your heart and life. As you allow God to develop the fruits of the Spirit in your heart and life, the purpose for your life takes on a deeper meaning. Reading your Bible everyday, praying to God, seeking Him with all your heart, developing His fruits of the Spirit, and getting to know Him . . . these are the best decisions you can make while going through grief. Studying His principles and making the decision to allow Him to change your heart will reap benefits that can't even be comprehended. God is totally worth pursuing, there is no greater relationship on earth! He is the only One with the ability to heal a broken heart and to truly make life brand new. God's magnificent ability to heal you of your pain, while restoring your life and joy, is a treasured gift from above. God, life, and wellness are worth pursuing—God will strengthen you and offer you healing so pursue Him with all your heart.

Jeremiah 33:6-9, *"But now take another look. I'm going to give this city a thorough renovation, working a true healing inside and out. I'm going to show them life whole, life brimming with blessings. I'll restore everything that was lost to Judah and Jerusalem. I'll build everything back as good as new. I'll scrub them clean from the dirt they've done against me. I'll forgive everything they've done wrong, forgive all their rebellions. And Jerusalem will be a center of joy and praise and glory for all the countries on earth. They'll get reports on all the good I'm doing for her. They'll be in awe of the blessings I am pouring on her."* (MSG)

God has the power to reveal to you how to live a true whole life, a life brimming with blessings. He *can* restore you and rebuild your broken heart and life, as you continue seeking Him with all your heart, mind, will, and emotions. His grace is sufficient to renew your heart and spirit. While going through grief or loss, the opportunity to go through renewal takes place. You find that living in the moment becomes of great importance. While going through grief, it is too painful to continually live in the past. Living in the moment opens a pathway to making the daily decision to live in the present. Going through a difficult life experience opens your heart and soul to truly appreciate even the smallest moments and experiences in life. While living in the moment, wellness begins to take over. You then will have the ability to truly appreciate all of the senses God has blessed you with. God instructs us in His Word to become child-like in our faith. What if every time you experience God in day to day life, you choose to live in the present moment through new eyes, like a child? When you enter into a friendship with God, in child-like faith, and begin living life to the fullest, all of the senses God has blessed you with will begin to take on a whole new meaning, because you are savoring every moment and every good thing in your life. Psalm 34:8, *"Taste and see that the Lord is good. Oh, the joys of those who take refuge in him!"* (NLT) It is possible to live in the moment, savoring God and every daily experience He blesses you with, so you are newly able to live life to the fullest.

Incorporating wellness is an excellent way to create a new life of meaning. When faced with grief or loss, you have the opportunity to take a step back and self reflect on the entirety of your life. You're able to see with clarity what has been great in your life, what's been bad in your life, what has worked, and what has not. During times of self reflection, you may feel unsettled about the twists and turns your life has taken. At that point, don't become bitter or discouraged. If you have the breath of life, you still have the power to change your life. If you don't like where you're at in life or who you've become, why not change it? Talk to those you admire, or who you deem successful, and ask them what principles they live their life by. If you are realizing that you have wasted a portion of your life, you do not have to continue to waste it. Think of how you truly want to live life then take the necessary steps to make it happen. Are you upset that through your grief you have allowed yourself to become physically unfit or unhealthy? Seek out the help you need to regain physical and nutritional wellness. Take daily walks, join a gym, or find ways to live a healthy life by reading or looking up health resources. Are you discouraged by a business or relationship failure? You do not have to define your life by your loss, grief, or failures—those are things or situations that happened *to* you, *they are not who you are.*

Life is a myriad of choices and decisions, and the good news is that you are free every single day to make new decisions and choices. You do not have to stay stuck in any situation. Every day is a brand new gift to you from God. It's never too late to reinvent any facet of your life, to make your life be of greater quality, or to pursue a long lost goal or dream. Use each and every day to live life fully, to better yourself and those around you, and to create a life that you love to live. Starting today, create new goals and write down the things you'd like to accomplish throughout the rest of your life. Think about what you want your life to be, the goals you want to accomplish, the successes you'd like to achieve, and the activities you would like to do. Create a Bucket List and challenge yourself to meet a goal or accomplish something you want to do every single day, regardless of any situation or feeling you are experiencing. Creating a Bucket List tremendously helped me through my grief. When I created my goals for my Bucket List, I made a decision to accomplish at least one goal every single day, regardless of how I felt for the day. My Bucket List currently has over 100 goals or things I want to accomplish and includes every aspect of life. I made the decision to create a Bucket List to hold myself accountable to not waste life . . . I don't want to get to the end of my life and realize I wasted it. Make the decision to take care of yourself, set goals, and incorporate wellness, whether life is good at the moment or falling apart. Take the necessary time while going through grief to fix anything in your life that you know isn't healthy. You may need to seek counseling from a pastor, nutritionist, Christian psychologist, or other professional. Do whatever you need to do to regain and develop optimal wellness for yourself. You may have had no control over the loss that knocked your breath and life out of you—but you do have a choice when it comes to your health, wellness, goals, and future. Make the decision to get your breath and life back! No, your life will not be the same, but there is still hope for your future! Life will definitely be different, for it can never be the exact same. Grief and loss may forever change your life and who you are—but what if life can eventually be better . . . or even great? Now is the time to take an inventory of your life, set goals, incorporate wellness, better your health, and make a Bucket List so that you will keep yourself accountable to live life to the fullest starting today!

After going through loss, you have absolutely no power over the past, but you do have the power to choose how you want to spend your future. Something my other sister that is still living says all the time is, *"Step by step, I can do this."* Step by step, *you* can do this! Starting right this moment, you have the power to choose, step by step, to create a fulfilling life that is filled with peace and joy. No, it may not be your former life, but you have the ability to create a new life filled with new meaning, new memories, new traditions, and new opportunities. Will there be tears, frustration, or sadness along the way? Yes, but keep making a conscious daily decision to get your breath back and truly live life! Life may have knocked the breath out of you *but* it doesn't mean that you don't deserve to learn how to breathe again. Choose to live life to the fullest in spite of your loss in every way you are able to. Do not waste your life for you still have purpose and a hope! With your life falling apart, now is the time to begin rebuilding a new life. It might be hard, challenging, uncomfortable, difficult, or heartbreaking, but you deserve to create a life filled with joy, love, peace, comfort, and memories. You can rebuild a new life while still treasuring your previous memories and never forgetting your loved one. So many times, we believe that moving forward is moving away from our loved one's memory. Moving forward *is not* forgetting your loved one, or your previous memories or life with them—moving forward *is* making the decision to live life for God, treasuring and remembering your loved one, living life in your loved one's honor, and respecting the life you currently have by choosing not to waste it. I'm not suggesting that the primary reason in striving to live and enjoy life is our deceased loved one's memory. Every life is valuable and deserves to have wellness, regardless of our loss. Our life is a precious gift from God and ultimately we should live our life for Him and in honor of Him. There is a purpose and a place for living our life to honor our loved ones, but the ultimate purpose for living, loving, and enjoying life to the fullest is because God created our lives, He loves us, and He has a purpose and plan for us. He is more than deserving of our total love and devotion.

While rebuilding your life, be prepared for the challenges of holidays. It is important to realize that upcoming special occasions, birthdays, anniversaries, holidays, and other important dates may be difficult to celebrate. You may need to create new traditions, and celebrate holidays in a totally new way, with a new approach for a period of time . . . and that's okay.

Be prepared that emotions may be heightened on holidays, special days, and occasions. Be sure to have a solid support system surrounding you on those days so they can offer you love, encouragement, and comfort. Invite family and friends over, telling them beforehand that you are struggling and you are in need of extra support. Some of you may need the extra support of family and friends, while some will prefer to spend holidays, special days, and occasions by yourself in peaceful solitude. Whatever is helpful and comforting to you and your family is what you must do.

Since my sister died on Thanksgiving, I really didn't enjoy that holiday for several years. It was very painful to try to have a traditional Thanksgiving dinner so our family decided to go to a Thanksgiving buffet at a restaurant for several years. It didn't change the fact that it was Thanksgiving Day but it was exactly the change we needed to take the steps to be able to eventually enjoy the holiday of Thanksgiving once again. We usually celebrate with a traditional Thanksgiving dinner, but every now and then we go to a buffet just because we enjoy it. You may find that holidays are difficult for the first few years after your loss. Depending on your loss, you may go through the events of your loss for years to come. There is never a Thanksgiving morning that I don't go through the events of the Thanksgiving Day that my sister died. The first couple of years, I'd become so upset that I'd be physically sick while crying and not be able to sleep. After a period of time, the crying transitioned into being able to peacefully sleep and asking God to tell my sister *"Happy Thanksgiving and Happy Home-going"* for me. I have truly been able to celebrate Thanksgiving the last several years and I enjoy celebrating Thankfulness with a brand new perspective.

I believe that holidays can be challenging because there is pressure from family and friends to "get on with life" and some may even try to make you feel morbid if you attempt to remember your loved one. It's natural to want your loved one to be remembered and honored, especially on a holiday, since holidays are the special premium days of the year.

Holidays can certainly be a challenge, but there are numerous heartfelt ways to honor deceased loved ones in your holiday memories. We grieved heavily the first Christmas after my sister's death, as her absence was very much felt. A very special and heartfelt gesture that we decided to do that first Christmas was to still set a place setting for my sister and simply light a candle on her plate. We painfully understood that she wasn't physically there, but it was a special experience to acknowledge her value, what she meant to us, and to honor her life.

When going through grief, it is sometimes confusing to know how to approach holidays. Juggling the conflicting ideas of celebrating holidays during grief can be frustrating. On one hand, you may feel as though you should honor traditions, but on the other hand, you may feel like not celebrating at all. I remember having a conflict of feelings about how to celebrate holidays. While growing up, Christmas before my sister's death was a time of great fun. My mom always went all out decorating our house, baking treats, and making sure we watched every Christmas special that was on TV. Some of my best memories as a child were because my fun mom knew how to celebrate holidays best! After going through my sister's death, we chose to make the holidays a very special and fun time, in spite of how we felt. At the time of my sister's death, she left behind daughters who were 10 months old, 2 years old, and 3 years old, and my son was also a toddler. We didn't want my son and nieces to remember holidays as a somber, sad time. It was hard at times, because I really wanted to just cry on some holidays, and I usually did after I had gone to bed—but it wasn't fair to my son or nieces to be robbed of having special holiday memories of joy, so we focused on making the holidays extra special for them. As time went by, holidays became easier to handle, and even truly joyful again. With some grief experiences, holidays will still be a special time that you are able to naturally celebrate. With other grief experiences, you may need to take a more relaxed approach to the holidays. Several years after my sister's death, celebrating the holidays became challenging again. In addition to grief we had already experienced one particular year, my sister's second fiancé also passed away. My sister's fiancé was very close to all of our family. He and my sister had been good friends for many years before they began dating, and they dated for 6 years before becoming engaged. He had been on several family vacations, and attended most family gatherings, so losing him was truly like losing a family member. The first Christmas after his death was hard on our family, and harder on my sister. In previous years, we always took the time to make holidays very special—but this particular year, we responded differently. Since my son and nieces were adults, we didn't have to be as concerned for the fun part of the holidays. We still enjoyed the holidays, and made many special memories, but this time the holidays were much more relaxed. We took the time to go through our grief and didn't place any unnecessary pressures on ourselves. We made the decision to care more about each other than the holiday festivities. Instead of running 100 miles-an-hour being busy, we treasured times sitting by the Christmas tree and fireplace, drinking hot chocolate, and enjoying spending time with each other. While we still watched the fun TV specials, we also watched Hallmark Christmas movies that had meaningful story lines. We still had fun and enjoyed the holidays, and even did many of our usual traditions, but we didn't put unnecessary pressure on ourselves to have the "perfect" Christmas. We instead allowed ourselves the freedom to grieve and to enjoy a relaxed holiday.

Going through grief definitely increases a person's capacity to feel things on a much deeper level, whether that is feeling sadness, anger, love, or appreciating even the smallest joys in life. It brings about change as well as a keen loyalty to old traditions. There are many new traditions that my family and I have created in response to our grief, and we also still love doing some of the old traditions we once enjoyed with our loved ones. I have found that it helps to keep a loved one's memory alive by still enjoying old traditions. Sometimes we'll combine old traditions and add a new twist to them too. For example, the Christmas before my dad died, he, my mom, my siblings, and I got into our pajamas and drove around looking at Christmas light displays. It's one of the last memories I have of my dad and it's a much treasured memory. Ever since my son was born, we get into our pajamas and drive around to look at Christmas lights every year. We included a new tradition of always bringing hot chocolate with us and after we get home, we eat Christmas cookies and watch a Christmas movie. This tradition is so dear to my heart because this tradition was inspired by my dad. My dad passed this fun tradition on to me and I hope my son will do this tradition with his children in the future as well.

For me, it has been very helpful to find ways to honor my loved ones, incorporating the special traditions we had shared together, and purposefully celebrating holidays and life. At first, it is truly hard to discover and implement new ways of celebrating traditions and living life without loved ones. It feels wrong, eerie, and tempts you to feel guilty, but we must remember this: *our loved one would not want us to feel sad or guilty for the times we celebrate, smile, or laugh. They would want us to smile, celebrate, and laugh as much as we can.* It brought them joy while they were here on earth so why do we think our loved ones would now want us to deny ourselves these great things in their death . . . they wouldn't want us to deny ourselves a full joy-filled life.

Think of a memory you enjoyed with your loved one. Is there a way that you can honor that special memory with friends or family that are presently in your life? Are there any new memories or traditions that you would like to enjoy? Is there a way to take an old tradition and bring it to life in a fresh new way?

Although honoring my loved ones through living life, celebrating holidays, and traditions was very helpful and meaningful, that is not what has filled my life and heart with ultimate joy. It relieved my grief significantly to honor my loved ones, and to allow myself to enjoy holidays, but I was able to enjoy life and holidays to the fullest after looking at life, holidays, and celebrations through an eternal perspective. When you realize what life and holidays are truly about, and honor the Reason for them, you are clearly able to truly celebrate, regardless of situations of grief. For example, if we were to celebrate Christmas primarily for the commercialized or fun facets of the holidays—Santa Claus, sugar cookies, toys, gifts, Christmas carols, reindeer, etc—it would be very difficult to celebrate Christmas after a loved one dies because the focus is primarily set on fun and a worldly perspective. But when we celebrate the true Reason for Christmas—Jesus and His birth—we are still able to fully celebrate because our focus is set on an eternal perspective. When our family celebrates Christmas, or any other holiday, we celebrate all the fun aspects, but our primary focus is God.

Grief enriches your relationship with God, your ability to savor life and live life to fullest, and develops a more powerful testimony. We do not have to stay stuck in our grief. We CAN have a new freedom to truly live life. We all have a life story and our life story contains many chapters. We will never forget the chapters we have been through, but there are many chapters to come. God is faithful to reveal His new purposes for our lives as we trust Him in moving forward. Moving forward does not mean that we will forget about our loves ones or our loss. How could we? Our loved ones will always be a part of our lives and they will forever be tattooed onto our hearts. After we thoroughly grieve, and as we choose to live life to the fullest, we make a declaration that our grief will not control our lives. Our lives are precious and are deserving of fully experiencing life.

Isaiah 43:18-19, *"Forget the former things; do not dwell on the past. See, I am doing a new thing! Now it springs up; do you not perceive it? I am making a way in the wilderness and streams in the wasteland."* (NIV) God will make a way for you to enjoy life, to take you from the barrenness of grief into the streams of life He has planned for you. God truly desires to give you life in its absolute fullness. I know it's hard, but living life fully will offer your heart an intense healing that you can't even begin to comprehend. One of the best ways we can honor a loved one is to truly enjoy life. We need to rediscover the activities that we once loved, and it is also okay to honor our loved ones by doing the activities that they once loved. I still honor my loved ones by doing the little things that I know they would have enjoyed doing. Doing activities that I know they would have enjoyed is a way that I choose to honor them. My sister loved to bake, go on vacations, and spend time doing fun things. I honor her memory by baking every week and giving the baked goods to those that God guides me to. I love honoring my loved ones by living life to the fullest. As I live life fully, I imagine my sister looking down from heaven and saying, *"Wow! I know you guys miss me. Thank you for loving me so much while I was on earth. It means so much to me that I was valuable to you, that you hurt so badly from my death, but please smile! Love life and live it like I would be doing if I had the chance again. Thank you so much for having fun with my girls and loving them for me since I'm not there to. I miss them and love them so much! Since I can't spend time with them and love them on earth, do it for me! I'll see all of you when you get up here and we are going to have a blast talking about everything. I am going to be so mad if I find out that all you did was cry or sit around being depressed. You know* how much I loved life, you know how much I loved family and doing things with all you guys . . . so get up and go celebrate life while you can! NOW!!!*" That is exactly what my sister would be saying if she was here. That's also what your loved one would be saying, *"Get up, go live life! I know it's hard, I know you miss me! I love you for missing me! If you can't find the strength to live life for yourself, then please live life in my honor for me!"*

I love what Psalm 51:7-15 says, *"Soak me in your laundry and I'll come out clean, scrub me and I'll have a snow-white life. Tune me in to foot-tapping songs, set these once-broken bones to dancing. Don't look too close for blemishes, give me a clean bill of health. God, make a fresh start in me, shape a Genesis week from the chaos of my life. Don't throw me out with the trash, or fail to breathe holiness in me. Bring me back from gray exile, put a fresh wind in my sails! Give me a job teaching rebels your ways so the lost can find their way home. Commute my death sentence, God, my salvation God, and I'll sing anthems to your life-giving ways. Unbutton my lips, dear God; I'll let loose with your praise."* (MSG) This passage of scripture sums it up. As I was going through grief, I took the truths of Psalm 51 and personalized this passage of scripture into a declaration as I began living life to the fullest. My declaration was: *"God, create in me a clean heart, a heart that can see from Your eternal perspective. Heal and restore my heart and my joy so that I can have the ability to truly enjoy You and life. Yes, there will still be blemishes in my soul as I recover from my grief, but overlook them with Your compassion as I seek you for total healing. Give me the grace to truly find and live a new way of life. Take the chaos of my grief and shape it into a beautiful purpose as You create every facet of my new life. The things I have been through have threatened to destroy me and have harmed my ability to enjoy life but do not look at me as worthless or discardable. I need You to breathe Your holiness into me and mold me into Your image. Bring me out of the darkened exile of my grief and revive me . . . renew me with fresh life. My grief has made me feel as though I am dead but can't die, it truly has felt like a death sentence. Raise me from the death sentence of grief so that I may truly live and love life once again. Restore to me the joy of salvation and I will tell others of what You reveal to me through my trials, praying that they will find their way to your heart through my testimony. Show me Your life-giving ways, teach me to truly live life, and give me a voice where grief attempted to silence me then I will give You all of the glory and all of the praise. I will praise You abundantly, Lord. Change my heart so that You are my highest and greatest treasure."* I truly believe that God allows us to go through loss and trials so He can teach us what life is truly about. With every lesson we learn from Him, we then are able to treasure life more and help others through their life challenges and loss. I also believe that some losses we go through in life will be allowed to sift our lives of the things we treasure above God. Some of the losses I have experienced have shown me the hidden idols I have had in my life. God wants us to make Him our highest treasure . . . He is to be our life and our greatest Love above everyone and everything. All that is given to us by God: family, friends, belongings, opportunities, things . . . everything . . . it is all given so we may praise Him and His goodness for His purposes and His ultimate glory. When we properly view God's blessings of people and things in our lives, we begin to have the ability to view everything from an eternal perspective. We also begin to see the need to: live a life of ultimate wellness, never miss an opportunity to live life, love others, and use the gifts and talents God has bestowed on us.

Make the previous declaration and the following commitment to God, yourself, your loved one, and for your remaining loved ones: *"I am going to experience Christ so much that He becomes my greatest treasure . . . He is going to become most important in my life so that I may experience life with Him to the fullest. I am going to do whatever it takes to get my breath back with God's help. I am going to live life to the fullest, make new memories, love life and others to the best of my ability, and never waste an opportunity to enjoy life. I will allow God to use me to make a difference in the lives of others. With God's help, I choose to experience Him and life to the fullest. I will learn from my grief, loss, and trials and seek God's heart daily as He guides and directs my life. I will not go through my grief or live my life in vain. I will from this day forward live a life of oxygen!"*

I hope as you have read this book you realized God's love and concern for you. Continue to seek His heart all the days of your life . . . He truly cares for you and loves you. May you bask in His love, for He truly is the ultimate Oxygen in getting your breath back after life knocks it out of you.

"Heavenly Father, thank you so much for You, family, friends, wellness, and traditions. Help me to see the good in my life and help me to embrace it and make the most of it. Lord, some holidays are so painful. Please heal my heart so that I may once again look forward to special occasions and holidays. Give me Your grace to create new traditions and to not be so hard on myself. Grant me the gift of good, solid relationships with my family and friends. If I need to find a church home, guide and direct me to the one that You know is best for me and my family. Lord, help me to incorporate wellness into every facet of my life. Bring health to my body, soul, and spirit. Heal my family, my marriage, and myself where healing is needed. Help my family and me to bond and draw close together and not to isolate ourselves from each other. Give each of us Your grace to not take life for granted, but to make the most of each and every opportunity. Lord, I praise you for the gifts of You, life, marriage, my children, family, church, friends, and community . . . all were designed by You to be enjoyed to the fullest. Show me how I can best enjoy and delight in each of these gifts from You today and in the days to come. Lord, please heal my heart. I love You, Lord, and thank You for all You have done for me. Continue to help me to fully get my breath back that life knocked out of me. Give me the grace to live a life filled with you, my ultimate OXYGEN. In Jesus Name I pray, Amen."

3 Oxygens

1. Consider the traditions you have in your family. What old or new traditions can you implement to make holidays more meaningful?

2. Make a Bucket List filled with goals, dreams, things you'd like to do, vacations you'd like to go on, etc. Having a Bucket List is a powerful motivator to not waste life. It will keep you accountable to fully live life in times of discouragement. Life is designed by God to be enjoyed so make a Bucket List to ensure you do.

3. Incorporate wellness into your everyday life. Speak to your doctor about nutrition, exercise, and wellness then follow his advice. Ensure your wellness and your family's wellness by spending time with God, eating right, practicing proper hygiene,

exercising, and enjoying life. Take time everyday to do something that you enjoy then take time to relax. God, family, friends, wellness, health, nutrition, exercise, enjoyment, traditions, grief recovery, and relaxation are all facets of living a life well. All of these will help you to get your breath back after life knocks it out of you.

End Matter/Appendices

A Child Loaned by Edgar A. Guest

I'll lend you for a little time,
A child of Mine," He said,
"For you to love the while she lives,
And mourn for when she's dead.
It may be six or seven years,
Or twenty-two or three,
But will you, till I call her back,
Take care of her for Me?
She'll bring her charms to gladden you,
And should her stay be brief,
You'll have her lovely memories,
As solace for your grief.
I cannot promise she will stay,
Since all from earth return,
But there are lessons taught down there,
I want this child to learn.
I've looked this wide world over,
In My search for teachers true,
And from the throngs that crowd life's lanes,
I have selected you;
Now will you give her all your love,
Not think the labor vain,
Nor hate Me when I come to call,
And take her back again?"
I fancied that I heard them say,
Dear Lord, Thy will be done,
For all the joy Thy child shall bring,
The risk of grief we'll run.

We'll shelter her with tenderness,
We'll love her while we may,
And for the happiness we've known,
Forever grateful stay.
But should the angels call for her,
Much sooner than we planned,
We'll brave the bitter grief that comes,
And try to understand.

61903540R00109

Made in the USA
Columbia, SC
27 June 2019